# Twisted Vines

An Autobiography of an Ex-Nun

Copyright © 2014 Patricia Ann Dudkiewicz

All rights reserved.

ISBN-10: 1495499782
ISBN-13: 978-1495499784

## DEDICATION

*I* dedicate this book to my husband Chet.

Also to my two sons, Steve & Mike

and my grandchildren:

McKinney (Mac)
Lauren
Ana
Colton
and
Griffin

whose lives would not have existed if I had not made the

very difficult decision to leave the Convent.

# Table of Contents

A SONG IN MY HEART ............................................................................... 1
A PEN IN MY HAND .................................................................................. 3
MY CORTISONE PARTY ............................................................................ 7
"THE BIBLE DISCOVERS ME" .................................................................. 11
PARTY PERFECT ........................................................................................ 14
PROPHECIES .............................................................................................. 16
THE SPUNK OF PIONEER WOMAN ...................................................... 20
REAL POVERTY – PHYSICAL & SPIRITUAL ........................................ 22
MY ARRIVAL ON EARTH ......................................................................... 25
THE TIMES WE LIVED IN ........................................................................ 28
LIFE BEGINS TO UNFOLD ...................................................................... 32
A SURPRISE VISIT ..................................................................................... 36
THERE IS ANOTHER WORLD! ............................................................... 39
I HAVE A DREAM! .................................................................................... 42
A NEW WORLD ......................................................................................... 44
BACK TO DISCORD .................................................................................. 48
WE CARRY OUR OWN BAGGAGE ......................................................... 51
THE GREEN LIGHT AND SULPHURIC SMELL OF LIGHTNING ..... 54
RE-ENTERING THE CONVENT .............................................................. 58
A DEVOTION THAT ABSORBED MY LIFE .......................................... 61
AT LAST – A BRIDE OF CHRIST ............................................................. 63
CHRISTMAS IN MY LIFE ......................................................................... 66
THE JOY OF HOLIDAYS .......................................................................... 68
THE HILARITY OF LOOKING BACK AT REALITY ............................ 71
FUN DAYS .................................................................................................. 75
HELL ON EARTH ...................................................................................... 79
LIKE FOAM – FUN RISES TO THE TOP ................................................ 85
ONCE MORE – I LIVE! .............................................................................. 90
LOOKING BACK ....................................................................................... 93
AND A COOKING WE WILL GO! ........................................................... 96
TALES OUT OF SCHOOL ......................................................................... 99
ALL OF LIFE IS A GIFT! ........................................................................... 103
WARM UP IN THE OCEANS OF MY SOUL .......................................... 107
REMINISCING ........................................................................................... 110
OH, THE SOLACE OF NATURE! ............................................................ 114
FINAL VOWS ............................................................................................. 120
THE DEFEAT CALLED DEPRESSION ................................................... 124
ISN'T THERE ANOTHER WAY? ............................................................. 126
MORE REMINISCING .............................................................................. 129

| | |
|---|---:|
| THE END OF A DREAM | 134 |
| FROM CHRYSALIS TO COCOON | 137 |
| LOOKING BACK ON EDUCATION | 140 |
| SEARCHING FOR A JOB | 142 |
| PERSONAL STRUGGLES | 145 |
| ENTERING THE WORLD OF MEN | 148 |
| MEETING CHET | 150 |
| ROMANTIC CONFUSION | 153 |
| MY LOVE GROWS! | 157 |
| THIS MAN IS NOT A FIGHTER | 160 |
| THE PRIDE AND JOY OF MY LIFE | 164 |
| WE BUY OUR OWN COTTAGE | 168 |
| THE FOUR SEASONS | 175 |
| SNAKES ALIVE! | 182 |
| NATURE ENTERTAINS US | 189 |
| OH FOR A SON'S ADULATION | 191 |
| MOM RETURNS TO HER GOD | 193 |
| TEMPORARY EMPLOYMENT | 199 |
| LADY SLIPPERS | 201 |
| SUPER MARIO BROTHERS | 206 |
| RETREATS | 209 |
| ARE YOU HIRING PEOPLE? | 212 |
| THE OTHER SIDE OF THIS DRY DESERT | 217 |
| THE PAIN IN OUR LIFE | 219 |
| PAIN, PAIN, PAIN | 221 |
| CHANGE IS INEVITABLE | 224 |
| WE ARE THE CHURCH | 227 |
| GRADUATIONS AND WEDDINGS | 229 |
| BIRTHS AND BAPTISMS | 233 |
| FUN STORIES NOT TOLD BEFORE | 242 |
| OUR WOOD LOT AND MAPLE SYRUP | 248 |
| TRYING TO DULL THE PAIN | 253 |
| A NEW DREAM EMERGES | 260 |
| GRADUALLY WINDING DOWN | 264 |

# ACKNOWLEDGEMENTS

### ❧ *I'd like to thank:* ❧

❧My husband for his constant patience and encouragement.

❧Sister Agnes Fischer who never allowed our friendship to deteriorate in the last 60 years.

❧For my husband's niece, Kathy Kaminski, who has called, checked on us, shopped and run errands, picked up our mail and checked our house daily for years.

❧My editor Joanne Flemming for her hours of work.

❧Bea Seidl, a Green Bay author, who gave me a great deal of advice and encouragement.

❧And last but best of all, Lisa Devroy who walked into my life from seemingly nowhere. Without her work, optimism, and expertise, this book would simply not exist!

## PROLOGUE

One summer during the hot dog days of August, my husband cut down a wild grapevine that was growing in our cottage yard. It was too hot to work that day, so he lazily and somewhat aimlessly, sat at the picnic table and made a wreath. He wound it in and out, over and around. Our sons and I joked about it and picked on him for his great ability to make an ugly wreath.

His circle of twisted, sun-dried vine lay on the woodpile until at Christm___ ___he boys brought it home. After all Dad went throug___ ___ make it, we felt obligated to use it.

We ___ in a pot and wound several live green ivies around th___ ___ing a beautiful red bow, some Cardinal birds, an___ ___ries, we now have an astonishing center___

___shapen grapevine wreath. It's f___

___years in the Convent; ___Convent), and 45 ___. The three vocations: ___woven and twisted, braided ___able where one ended and the other began. There seems to be no beginning, no end to the circle – just like the wreath.

Upon adding the green growth of the three vines of life, and the colorful fruit of each vocation, the wreath has a dignity and inner glow of life and vitality, which are unique to it.

The events and thoughts in this book twist and turn and weave at will. They can't be separated. It's my piece in God's Mosaic of Life. Without that piece which is distinctly mine, the whole picture would be less rich.

This I've learned for sure. We may think that we know the path that God wants us to follow. Indeed, we may very well be right where He wants us to be. If we stray or take another road, our Good Shepherd will retrieve us.

Jesus, Our Good Shepherd, searches for us; broken, wounded, or dirty though we may be. He picks us up gently in His arms without causing us further pain. All we have to do is accept our own weakness, our own nothingness, and rest sorrowfully and repentantly in His arms. He will heal, mend, and strengthen us, if we just let Him.

We may not feel God's Presence. Blessed Mother Teresa of Calcutta spent her whole life without <u>feeling</u> the Presence of God.

Christ on the cross, the God – Man, who died to save us all from our sins, cried out "My God, My God, Why have you abandoned me?" As a Man, He knows our feelings of abandonment. Let us turn to the magnetism of the Father, even if we can't feel Him.

# One

## A SONG IN MY HEART

God has written a song into my heart that must be sung!

I used to have a beautiful high soprano singing voice. Years have passed – hormones have been depleted. I now sing bass. Like my singing voice, my life has known its highs and lows, but the beat still goes on.

My song is blowing in the tree tops of my mind. Sometimes, the ballad, like the trill of the song sparrows high in the pines in spring, seems to be too loud.

I think that I simply must tone down the volume for the sheer lust of life is almost unbearable. It seems that I could burst if I allowed the crescendo to continue.

The song drums on, through the frogs who sing so loudly, soon after they crawl out of the freezing muck and snow, around the lake. They all clamor in a dinning chorus – calling, inviting, and outdoing each other, in a tremendous outpouring of life, love and melody.

There is a wide creek bed and a surrounding swampy area leading into the lake where our cottage is located. On certain mysterious, warm, humid nights in July, the fireflies all hatch, glow and mate. On a peak night, when our sons were little, we had to hold them in our arms because they were afraid that they would be burned. The fireflies resembled a river of burning candles for as far back as the eye could see, into the dark night forest.

Each of us contains our own light. No one else but us can produce the distinctive clarity of light that emanates from our soul. Let us not waste life cursing the darkness. If our own light is lit, darkness is not existent within our aura.

Man those are big toads! And can they trill in spring!

# Two

## A PEN IN MY HAND

For 14 years, I was a food demonstrator in one of the most wonderful supermarkets on earth, Copp's. I once spent two days cooking a recipe that involved boiling a sauce containing raspberry, vinegar, and mustard. Because I was serving hundreds of people, I made the batches in triplicate. Being handicapped with severe arthritis, I walked with canes and didn't move often. Consequently, I sat at my demo table, physically close to my product and cooking equipment. The area was rather enclosed and the ventilation was not optimum. It disturbed my respiratory system but I had no idea that it was harming me.

I began to have a terrible breathing problem. Upon going to the doctor two or three days later, I was told that my entire bronchial system was severely burned. He described it as a major burn without lymph or skin coverage. Any environmental change could agitate the condition and make it worse. Infection was a serious possibility.

Two and a half weeks before Christmas there was a probability that my live tree couldn't be used. We perhaps could not use the fireplace, candles, spicy or aromatic foods, etc., etc., etc.

I was put on forty milligrams of prednisone each morning, antihistamines, ventilators, and cough medicine with codeine. Still I was gasping for air like a fish in a polluted tank. Upon my returning to the doctor, my prescription for prednisone was doubled.

Taking eighty milligrams of prednisone a day resulted in my feeling like I was being strung taut by a wire puller. My life and thoughts raced ahead of me like a speeding Amtrak train. Normally, if left alone, I could sleep ten to twelve hours at a time. Arthritis depressed me and fatigued my energy. While taking the cortisone, I was very lucky if I could sleep two or three hours a night.

During this illness I was afraid of death – knowing that in many ways I have failed to truly live the life God has bestowed within me. I was painfully aware that even my breath was just a borrowed gift from God. I was brought face to face with the awareness that I might lose my voice entirely and no longer be able to vocally praise God – soprano or bass! Honestly I was afraid that I might no longer be able to speak or sing.

Facing the above threat brought about a new, poignant, illumination. God has given me a great inherited talent, which I also must account for in heaven. I'm a born writer. When inspiration hits, ink flows from my hand onto paper like a bird's song in the air.

So, dear God; with a song in my heart and a pen in my hand, I shall write my autobiography! I am opening my life and my soul to all who read. Perhaps someone who thinks life is not worth living will read this testimony to life itself, and find his or her own freedom to breathe and take nourishment and shine.

Each human being is capable, with God's grace, of transmitting the light of God – the reflection of Christ – in a way only <u>that</u> human being can achieve. We can each be, like a facet of the Eternal Diamond, reflecting God's love and light and warmth back into a cold, dark, depressed world.

Christ said, "Seek and you shall find. Ask and you shall receive." He was talking to each of us today. We won't all find our answers in the same place. We're perhaps not all seeking the same things. Christ certainly doesn't answer us all in the same way. We often do not get the answer we expect and it's not found where we are looking. But He does answer us.

If we look carefully, and listen intently, our prayers are always answered. If we allow noise and confusion and selfishness to rule us, we'll never see or hear Christ speaking and touching us. He offers us the unconditional love of the Trinity. If we close our hearts, that love can never enter, but that is not the Creator's fault!

These were four inches tall when Steve got them in kindergarten. Twenty years later, they are 7 feet tall palm trees.

150 pieces of colored felt underneath cut leather outlines.

Christmas Village – a gift from Mike when he was 9.

# Three

## MY CORTISONE PARTY

People tell me that prednisone does unusual things to personalities. Some eat all the time, become anxious, depressed, angry, etc. I don't know exactly how it's affected me but I do know that it has pushed me over the edge of my own frozen precipice. I am feeling the freedom of the eagle to soar at will, on the currents of air high above the resistance of mundane earthly concerns.

I couldn't sleep. I'd lie awake with wild creative thoughts coursing through my brain and overloading the lifeblood racing through my arteries and veins. This resulted in what I have dubbed, "My Cortisone Party!"

My poor husband would be engaged in the sleep pattern of a normal human being, while I was out destroying the peaceful design of his quiet life.

I decided to have a party – one that I thought would be the Mother of all parties – at least for a relatively "poor" person of the late nineties.

At three a.m. in the morning, crazy invitational signs came to life. I invited all the employees and managers of my great super market to an open house: spouses, children, company, and significant others, etc.

I was incapacitated, not contagious or dead. I was on workman's compensation. I know that the idea of a party must have been questionable in some people's minds. If I couldn't work, how dare I have a party?

This was all conspired and put into motion without even the <u>tacit</u> approval of my sleeping husband. I probably deserved to be quarantined from normal people!

I spent nights contriving plans and writing notes to keep up with my racing mind. The last three nights before my Cortisone Party, I mixed spreads and dips and concoctions all night long. I could have served generous samples to all my store customers during a grand opening and still have had a refrigerator full of leftovers.

In the past my husband jokingly said, "If you were to die before me, I would head your obituary as "The Sample Lady returned to God. Samples will be served at the wake from 4:00 p.m. until 9:00 p.m." Everyone would come, ensuring that I would have a big funeral!

Jokingly in my mind at this time, I decided that I'd rather give out my own samples while I was alive and enjoy my own flowers.

When my husband woke up to the fact that all this was really going to transpire, he flew into action. I could possibly have three hundred people in our house between 10:00 a.m. and 12:00 midnight.

Everything had to be cleaned, dusted, and rearranged. Someone had to do it and obviously I was totally incapable of any physical activity! I have never been accused of being a good or even a fair housekeeper.

I'm a great cook and a good decorator. I'm very good at a lot of things, but let me tell you the word; "housekeeping" is not in my vocabulary. I doubt that it's even in the Webster Dictionary on my bookshelf!

I wasn't capable of working at the store; therefore I was rested and relaxed. The house was decorated fantastically – in my own artistic style. Some of these decorations, like my twenty-three year old son's seven-foot ceiling high, palm tree, with lights and teddy bears, would not be available another holiday season.

Steve is getting married soon. His new home has twelve foot ceilings. Thus, the plant could grow another five feet in his home.

Our house was singing its own song. We planned to clean the carpet as soon as we took down the live balsam tree and other decorations. It was an ideal party time, meaning to me, now or never!

The open house was to be spread over a fourteen hour period. Food, drink, games, social interchange – all would be available. Also, pool, pinball, artist corner, card tables, darts, and Nintendo were accessible. It was a well-planned party. I hired a friend to do my social duties, such as taking photos and having people sign a register. We were to have the fun of "re-living" our party.

The host and hostess were prepared down to the minutest detail! Forty people came. For the people who did come, I'm positive it was a good party. It certainly was for us. We had hours to get acquainted. All of us who were present shared the rooms full of love and heard the "song" being sung. This evening, as I sit and write, unable to sleep, I am clearly aware that the song is still afloat, bouncing off the walls.

The time span allowed anyone from any shift to fit the party into whatever schedule they were on, if they so wished.

God has blessed me. I am just a bumbler, but somehow I am aware that I am a human magnet. People like me – just as children loved me when I taught school. I'm sort of like a Pied Piper! So I know people intended to come. It was a wild, free, and unencumbering invitation.

As in the Bible story, the excuses began to flow. They didn't buy a cow, marry a wife, or bury an ass. Instead, "I didn't have a ride, had to work, and was too tired. Oh, it was Friday? I thought it was Saturday! I got company; I went out of town; I got drunk; couldn't get a baby sitter, had a fight with my spouse," etc., etc., etc.

Now, <u>think</u> with me: God on a grand scale has invited us all personally, unconditionally, to the unfathomable party of Eternal

Life. He's planned this grandiose celebration. He's given us each the garment of grace. He's <u>given</u> it. We don't need to work or pay for it; we must only don it and appreciate it.

How many of us will continue to make our million excuses and deliberately or carelessly not show up?

It's not God's fault if we miss the Eternal Celebration of Life. He invites us to His Party, but being the wonderful God that He is – He gave us Free Will – even God cannot make us participate in the greatest party of all times!

Our favorite Teddy bear holiday decorations.

## *Four*

## "THE BIBLE DISCOVERS ME"

As a nun, I read hundreds of spiritual books and used daily meditation books about the Life of Jesus. Every liturgy I ever attended had New and Old Testament readings – that being <u>every</u> day – sometimes two or three times a day. But I had to be a lay person of the Church for over twenty-five years before I discovered the beauty of the Living Wisdom of God in His personal Letter Book to us.

I read inveterately. Through the years I remember having felt distressed inside if I had been trapped alone, waiting even for five minutes without something in hand to read.

The thought would pop up every year or so – that it would be a shame if I read all my life and died without ever having read the greatest Book on earth.

In a lay people's retreat about 20 years ago, I was given a Bible, as were all the other retreatants. Circumstances were such that I knew – or <u>heard</u> God say in my heart, "Take and eat." He didn't say, "Read." He said, "This is My Body – Take and eat; This is My Blood, Take and drink." This is not <u>heresy</u>. This is my Awareness of the voice of God in my heart. I certainly receive the Body and Blood of my living, resurrected Lord Jesus in the Holy Eucharist at Mass.

However, the absorption of His Story Book within my soul makes Him seem ever so much more alive in the Sacrament of the Eucharist and in my daily life.

I have honestly spent recent years studying, meditating and reading nothing but the Bible. I have studied it hand in hand with the Catholic Collegeville Bible Commentary. I do not take the Bible literally. For my book it's not the details that count. It's the story or message that is important. I was a nun but I guess no one could ever make a "nun" out of me.

I apologize! In deepest respect to my individual nun friends, -- they would probably each say that! The world categorizes all of us. There really is no such thing as a NUN. They are each individuals, loving, serving and reacting to the love of God within their own souls. We are all sinners – we all struggle like every other human on earth. I believe, that the religious habit, unwittingly set us aside from the world, and from our own humanity, and left us protected but perhaps gasping for air – like I was doing several weeks ago without Cortisone when my body needed it. I still prefer a religious habit but it has its inherent downfalls. This book will ramble. I feel that the Holy Spirit is guiding my pen – and what and how He says it through my soul and personality is what you will get in this book.

I just woke up. My cortisone has been cut by half and miracle of miracles, I slept NINE hours last night! I woke up wanting to roll over and enjoy the luxury of sleep but thoughts were dancing in and out and around my head. I was cognizant of the Holy Spirit saying, come on Honey; you have a book to write!"

So – with the Holy Spirit blowing, this book will move forward. Wherever each of us is in life, the Holy Spirit whispers shouts, or roars at us, if necessary.

To live we need air. The Holy Spirit is the breath of God – the love of the Father for the Son. He is the love of the Son for the Father. Without love, babies die. Without love, adults go crazy or kill themselves or others. The Holy Spirit is the love or Breath of God. Please, my readers – Breathe!

This tree had 90 hand-crocheted snowflakes made by my niece, Carol.

## *Five*

## PARTY PERFECT

*B*ack to my <u>Cortisone Party!</u> It was spread over a fourteen hour period. Only one tenth of the people invited came. For those of us who attended, it smacked of a taste of Heaven. It was beautiful and quiet. Everyone had hours of time to leisurely get acquainted and share each other's love of life itself. I know those who attended felt and sang the song of life.

My party was perfect: I was prepared (with everyone's frantic help), to the hilt. If no one had come, it would have been O.K. and still perfect. Believe it or not, the situation was such that we had achieved our goal and we were completely content.

I ended up inviting some people from our companion store where I had previously worked. Everyone had bold, blatant access to several large printed invitations in the break room. This was a room everyone had to enter each day to punch in on a time card. It was impossible to miss the invitation notices. I was told that people spent their whole breaks reading and laughing about the wild invitations to this absolutely mind-boggling, unconditional party proposal.

They could bring their children or <u>anyone</u> else along, company included. As I was shopping for party food, I personally invited and had over one hundred people say, "Oh, yes, I'm certainly coming or will surely try. It sounds like a blast! I called people on different shifts that I didn't see but knew and felt a fondness for. I'm reiterating this to impress the awareness that this was not an impersonal invitation. Some outsiders from the store I worked for before even called and invited themselves. One said, "I'll come twice. I'll come in the afternoon and then again at night after bowling." He never showed!

Our party was wonderful. Forty people came.

Great care went into the planning and production of My Cortisone Party.

# *Six*

## PROPHECIES

*O*nce, years ago, during a retreat, a man had prophesied to me, "Someday your mouth will open. Maybe not soon," he said, "But it will open and you will be a powerhouse!"

And I thought, "Ya, right! You're nuts if you think I'll ever step out into the open and let people shoot at me and hurt me. I'm protected, fortressed, walled and inaccessible. No one will ever get to touch me in my inner soul, where anyone can discover that I feel, hurt, bleed, etc. Never again will <u>anyone</u> get into my inner sanctum, not in this lifetime. I've been hurt too much in the past. I won't ever love the world unconditionally again, because people walk over your mat, wipe their feet on you and leave their crud and dirt behind on your psyche."

Twenty years after these pages were written, I realize that this is what he was talking about; I now see this as the fulfillment of his prophecy. At the time, he prophesied I would never have foreseen writing a book. This book was written many years ago. Only upon rereading it, did I realize that my mouth has finally opened! I will publish this book!

I was helping give a Koinonia Retreat. Koinonia is a Greek word meaning "meeting Christ in Community." This was years after the above prophecy.

During one of the group chapel visits, a fellow leader who happens to be another Charismatic with the gift of prophecy, turned to me and said, "I have been given a message for you." She handed me a card upon which she had written down the message she had supposedly received for me. I am totally unacquainted with charisms. I know they're wonderful – it's just not within my natural bent of experience.

Now, this written message was handed to me. "I will turn up the heat. The glacier will melt and the Ice Princess will be set free!"

It was written on the back of a picture of Christ, with His head back, laughing joyfully.

The Prophetess said to me, "This doesn't make any sense to me. Maybe it means something to you. I was told to give you this message, and I've done that."

Way deep down, I knew what it meant. I wondered how anything on earth could possibly melt the glacier that was I.

I knew that it was a valid prophecy, but I surely didn't understand how it could ever come to pass. I even fretted with Mary the Blessed Virgin – "And it came to pass that a Child was born," etc.

My monologue would go, "Yeah, I know you trusted in God – I know nothing made sense to you and yet you said, "Your will be done!" – But this is <u>me</u>. "I'm just a dumpy, frozen, spirit paralyzed, old woman who is useless, and besides, it was <u>God</u>, talking to You, Mary!"

Kind of like the party thing – excuses, excuses, excuses! And my best, <u>all</u>-<u>encompassing</u> excuse was – but I'm married. I have a husband and sons. They would never understand a change in me! They'll pick on me, "kill" me, divorce me, and disown me! How do you like my <u>repertoire</u>? Unbeatable, isn't it?

Eighty milligrams of prednisone a day – Turned up the heat – Melted the glacier, and I, the Ice Princess, <u>have been set free</u>!

As I mentioned earlier, God said, "Ask and you shall receive!" He did not say when or how. If we don't <u>see</u> what we are looking at or

<u>hear</u> what we're listening <u>to</u>, -- or <u>mean</u> what we're asking for – we must not blame God if we think that He is not answering our prayers.

So my "Cortisone Party" is the beginning of my autobiography. I sat here the other evening and I absorbed the Song of Life. It was composed by God, implanted in My Soul and I felt Him say, "Play it!"

Somewhere, perhaps, this rendition of my song will mean something to someone else. I know so many people who think that they have messed up their lives – think that their life is not worth living. They turn down the volume or disconnect their own life energy – unplug their own existence, either by drugs, food, illicit sex, alcohol, divorce, or suicide.

We each have our very own song to sing. Let's raise our voices! While we're singing together, the noisy world will want to tune down our volume. With each of our spirit lights aglow – we'll banish the darkness around us!

My mother loved the comparison of life to a huge Mosaic. We each add our own color, shape, and distinction. If our piece, however, big or small, is missing in the Mystical Life Mosaic of Christ, the Whole Picture will be less perfect, the whole Song will be less enriching, less colorful and less fulfilling.

Each one of us, no matter how good or how bad we are, is as important to God as if we were the only child that He ever created.

Let's rise and sing our Song. The New Millennium of Life is ours and it's Worth Living!

# TWISTED VINES – An Autobiography of an Ex-Nun

*Jesus Laughing*

"Cheer up, don't be afraid . . . for the Lord our God has arrived to live among you. He is a mighty savior. He will give you victory. He will rejoice over you in great gladness; He will love you and not accuse you.
Is that a joyous choir I hear? No, it is the Lord himself exalting over you in a happy song."

Zephania 3:16-18

*I'm going to turn up the heat
The glacier will melt and
I will release the Ice Princess*

## Seven

## THE SPUNK OF PIONEER WOMAN

My mother told me after I had entered the convent that she and dad had lived several years with his father's mother. Apparently dad and his mother had a verbal agreement that if he helped her run the homestead farm, he and his wife were welcome to live with her. Mom certainly thought she was welcome there.

Dad and his younger brothers were sporadically building his log house on the other side of the river.

Four years later, three children had arrived. One day Mom could no longer stand the tension. There were five people too many in Grandma's house and she must have let Mom know.

Mom packed the baby, quilts, and food in the buggy and went down the hill – toddlers alongside. This was November 5!

She swept out the place as the sheep had been using it for shelter.

A couple men came down the hill with dad to insist mom go back up the hill for the night.

"No," she said, "I will not go there again until Granny invites me"!

Dad stayed with Mom overnight. The next morning a group of men showed up, at sunrise, to install doors, windows, beds, and a huge wood cook stove!

Several days later, Mom went up to Granny's pump for water. Granny came out and invited her and the kids in for tea and cookies.

Her words were, "Maude, that was the best thing you could have done! Now we can be friends!

I will always love my mother for her pioneer spunk. There were no worldly conveniences or compensations in her life.

Granny at a relative's house.

A four generation picture; Granny, Dad, my oldest sister Ethel, and her baby, Barbara. In the background is the home I was raised in.

# Eight

## REAL POVERTY – PHYSICAL & SPIRITUAL

My parents raised six healthy children in a one-room log cabin. We were a stone's throw from the bank of a river which was a very good trout stream back then. This home was cold and dirt-poor. There was no basement, no attic, no insulation, and no storm windows. I'm sure I'd be exaggerating if I said the house was thirty by thirty feet square.

There was no electricity, no telephones, no fans, or air conditioning.

It was built on the ground. In winter the wind whipped snow through the chinks in the logs, mom or dad would sweep it up with a broom or dustpan. The house was heated with wood that we sawed, chopped and aged. No amount of wood burned heated the floor!

We used an outhouse that seemed to be a mile away. At least it was past the pines in which lived a frightful great-horned owl, who loved to scare the hell out of you one way or another.

All of our water was obtained from a wooden, algae-laden barrel that was sunk into the creek for spring water.

Between the house and the spring was a very unsanitary barn. We usually had seven to eight cows. Two horses also took residence in that barn. Somewhere between the barn and the spring there always lurked a mean old gander and his gaggle of geese. If it weren't for Old Wolf, our aging German shepherd, one of us would surely have been pummeled to death by that overly hormonal bird. We also raised our own chickens and pigs.

We had very little money; we ate what we raised. None of us knew what store-bought clothes were. Mom made everything. There was a humongous garden, fish in the stream and endless woods full of berries, along with bear, wolves and deer and a lot of bobcats. Coyote howls filled the air on winter nights.

Every wild flower that Wisconsin owned was at our fingertips.

As I understand my family history, religion was always a source of contention. My father's mother was from Ireland. She married a Scotch Protestant in this country. They moved out onto homestead land, twenty-two miles from a town or church. Knowing Irish history, I'm sure her religious affiliation tended more toward fighting over religion, than living it.

My grandfather didn't give a damn about farm labor. As for grandmother, <u>she</u> was the farmer. Grandpa was a cheese maker. I got the idea that he became pretty much of a scapegoat for everything that was ever wrong with her world.

Grandma divorced Grandpa when he bought a set of World Book Encyclopedias. It is my understanding that it wasn't the purchase that was the "mortal sin" – actually reading them was the straw that broke the camel's back. Grandpa later became an itinerant Protestant street preacher in New York City.

My father, the first child in his family, was baptized a Catholic. His lifetime religious experience was solely religious family war. That can be great fun! Any disagreement regarding any problem in life can be turned into a religious battleground if the contestants wish to do it. I've witnessed this a hundred times at least in my lifetime.

So my father grew up Catholic in name – having no idea what that meant. One thing he was sure of – he should squelch any Protestant religious growth or movement in his immediate family.

At twenty-five, my father married my mother, who was seventeen and a devout Methodist. The war escalated! Not only was she Protestant – Dad was possessive, and this God-business had to go! Mom tried to give her six children a moral religious background. Morality, Dad was all for. Religion, he did his damndest to kill.

Dad was naturally a very good man. When I think back, I don't know how he could have been so good without supernatural motivation. He was frustrated with the life that he seemed to be imprisoned in and this often broke out into unreasonable anger. That and religious antagonism were basically the only faults I remember in him. He kept the last seven Commandments. It was the first three that were his undoing.

My father also had cousins who were Mennonite ministers in Illinois.

My mother's parents were good, talented, intelligent people. Their heritage was Irish and English. Grandpa was a logger and strangely enough, a writer. He had beautiful penmanship and practiced cursive writing styles. Grandma was a phenomenal dressmaker. Her house was always full of gorgeous wedding ensembles.

My Grandmother was a Methodist. Later, she joined Grandpa in his serious study of Christian Science.

Now, I've set up the background for my autobiography.

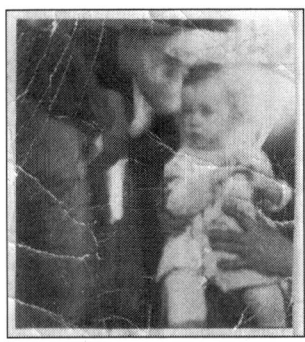

The only picture of.
me as a baby

I was 7 years old.
I was afraid of a neighbor's ram.

# Nine

## MY ARRIVAL ON EARTH

As best I have the story, and I've checked numerous times with my only living sibling who is now 88 and living in Georgia; my mother once again became pregnant. My oldest sister was eighteen and away making her own living. My other siblings were sixteen, fifteen, fourteen, twelve and nine – all of whom had been born at home.

One bitter November day, two months before I was supposed to be born, my mother went into eclampsic convulsions due to uremic poisoning.

She was in a coma for nine days in the hospital.

Once during this period Dad had gone home to check on the family. It was twenty-two miles from the hospital. He owned a 1929 Model T. During the night, a neighbor who had a telephone got the message that Mom was critical. She and the baby couldn't make it. Dad went into the hospital to find that a group of nuns had been praying all night long on their knees around her bed. Several days later, Mom awoke and said she was going to have her baby right there on that bed – that day. To the nun's relief, she did.

On November 20, 1934, I weighed in at three and a half pounds. I don't know whether they took very good care of me. They surely would have thought it was a waste. Dad told my brothers and sisters, before he brought me home that I looked like a skinned rat! When Mom left the hospital with me, the nun in charge of the Maternity Ward said, "Don't feel badly when your baby dies. You have six healthy children. Take care of <u>them</u>." How's that for reality?

Mom spent much of the winter in bed to keep me warm. She also said she carried me wrapped inside her clothing against her breasts. Later, there were references to keeping me in a box on the warming oven while she was cooking.

I wouldn't eat and if I did, I couldn't keep anything down. Dad went back to the doctor to ask for a different formula and the doctor said, "Man, it doesn't matter what you feed her, she can't possibly live, -- and if she does, she'll never be normal."

Now, you've all witnessed my living – the <u>normal</u> part has been questioned throughout the years by both me and others!

These were Depression years and in our neighborhood everyone was depressed. Dad worked on Roosevelt's W.P.A. so he could qualify for help when the baby came.

Mom asked for a special product called "Mellon's Baby Food." It had to be imported from England. It was somehow classified as pre-digested. Social services questioned why anyone had to have something that special. One look at the starving baby and they ordered it immediately.

At five months, I weighed seven pounds. When I was nine months old, there was a huge carbuncle on the base of my neck from rolling my head back and forth. The doctor who lanced it said that there was enough poison in it to kill a grown man. It was caused partially by the albumin poisoning that had been stored in my body before birth.

At a year old, I caught whooping cough. Mom said she'd get up in her sleep, grab me by the feet and shake me upside down to loosen the death grip of the phlegm.

In talking to my brother to see what he knew that I might not have been told, he exclaimed, "<u>I</u> remember <u>that</u>!" Shaking a fragile baby upside down had apparently imprinted a deep memory within him. He recalled that they had made some sort of a hood over the crib that I slept in and had to keep something burning under it, but he didn't know what it was. I think that mom told me it was sulphur.

As I was approaching age two, Mom used to put me outside in a playpen during nice summer days. The family had to have chicken for supper one night because one got too close to my play pen and our faithful dog, "Old Wolf" killed it in action. He was protecting me!

For some reason, God, man, and beast fought to keep me alive. I have always been like one with my mother. It seemed like the same blood coursed through our veins. I'm sure that struggle between the two of us for mutual survival was the reason or that unity.

The home I was raised in for eight years.
Grandma, Dad, my sister Ethel and her baby Barb.

My eighth grade graduation. I am on the left.

## Ten

## THE TIMES WE LIVED IN

Trouble was fermenting in Europe and Asia at this time. America tried to stay out of it. It was a period of grave concern for everyone.

My oldest brother, Art, had joined the CCC after high school. This was a program President Franklin Delano Roosevelt had developed to hire young men. It taught them electrical and carpentry skills plus discipline. They built roads through swamps and helped make parks.

My brother Roger was 17. I remember one afternoon when I was seven, a group of men coming out of the woods after cutting Christmas trees for sale. They were all crying.

The Japanese had invaded Pearl Harbor. It was December 7, 1941. This event would affect everyone.

Art voluntarily joined the Air Force. He was stationed in the United States for four years during which time he married. After the defeat of Guam, he and his wife lived there for three years. Again the Army used his mathematical talent.

During the war many products that Americans were familiar with were in frugal supply – tires, gas, shoes, flour, sugar, spices, leather, oil, to name a few. Many were rationed.

Roger got his draft notice on his 18th birthday. He had not yet graduated from high school. A year later he had gone through basic training and was sent to Germany. He was fighting near the Elbe River when he was shot through the neck. Within a year he was home.

The bullet went through his ear lobe and came out the other side. It missed his spine by an eighth of an inch. He is 88 now in 2014.

Ethel's husband Ray was too old for service. Helen's husband, Eric Henkel, was exempt from service. He ran a large farm. Had he gone to war, he'd have been fighting cousins. His parents came from Germany.

Kay and Nora's husbands worked in ammunition factories in Detroit.

I became my Dad's hired hand without pay. Anything a boy could do to help on the farm, I did. I had to feed the animals and clean up after them.

When fall came, by necessity, I helped kill, butcher and preserve pigs, cows, calves, rabbits, and sheep. The only means we had to preserve meat was to can it. Dad and I both helped with that. Mom did can mixed vegetables and meat with meat stock for soup that I loved. To this day I do not like canned meat.

We also used to have either one or two deer for food, obtained legally or otherwise. If you got caught you paid the price of a hefty fine. Farmers all killed deer for their meat. They ate the farmer's produce and he considered it his right to claim their meat.

It was 1940. The Great Depression was letting up a little. We had a little more money. Milk prices were up. We raised an acre of green beans for the government. I think they were for the Armed Forces. They were picked every day. We got 3¢ a lb. for picking.

I was very involved in 4H. This was an organization that gave farm children a chance to develop great pride in work they had to do any way. We worked all year. We displayed results at the county fair. We were awarded ribbons and subsequently money as prizes.

I displayed chickens, rabbits, sheep, insect collections, canned goods and bakery. We kept detailed records of the hours worked. This made us want to work. Thus parents were rewarded also.

At this time my parents decided to build a new home. They bought two homes that were going to be demolished and tore them apart to get lumber.

Mom, Dad, my maternal Grandpa and I built it. It turned out lovely but it had one drawback – the three small, constantly cold streams running in the basement to the river. The streams became our refrigerator.

Our basement was flooded whenever it rained hard or the river rose. The new house was always cold. Our heat was a potbellied stove in the living room, which heated the upstairs by way of a ceiling vent.

There were two bedrooms downstairs and one large one upstairs that held two full-sized beds. A porch enclosed the front of our house.

We had a pump and a sink in the kitchen. We still did not have electricity. Lighting was by kerosene lamps.

The all-time funniest thing that I ever saw was when I was a child and my father was mixing plaster for the walls in our new house. Days before, new windows had just been installed with the stickers still on them. Dad was mixing plaster on a frame on the floor. As he bent over with the hoe to pull the plaster forward, he rear-ended the window and it shattered. I was about seven years old at the time but I certainly knew better than to laugh!

Another time, I got swatted for spilling a glass of milk. Almost immediately after, Dad, in his frustration, turned and tipped a whole quart of milk off the table and all over the newly-painted wall. I was smart enough to know that that also wasn't funny.

TWISTED VINES – An Autobiography of an Ex-Nun

The new house finished in 1941.

Mom & Dad after working on building the new house one day.

# Eleven

## LIFE BEGINS TO UNFOLD

*I* lived in a <u>very</u> domineering, authoritarian atmosphere when I was growing up. My world was strictly structured. At fifteen, all my brothers and sisters had left home either temporarily or permanently. They had to grow up, get an education and go to work to support themselves.

My father was a good man but one jumped to his tune. Never would it have entered my mind to disagree or question a request. One anticipated everyone's wishes. There was no need to be told to do anything – unless it was a new development or there was a reason for instruction.

Because of the need to get out and make one's own living, I have absolutely no memory of brothers and sisters at home except for the brother next to me. By the time I came along, he had been nicknamed, "Red"; no man on earth could have been more adored by his nine-year younger sister than Red.

My memories of "Red," are even minimal, but so alive! He was the cleanest, fastest, "bestest" raspberry, blueberry, and blackberry picker on earth. He certainly caught the largest brook trout that ever came out of our trout stream. I recall walking over the bare wooden floor, through the old rickety back-screen door, onto the hot, finely pulverized area where the chickens dusted their feathers. Mom had just made bread and "Red" handed me my share of a fresh loaf. I can still feel the heat and smell that bread. I even remember I wished that he had put butter and sugar on it.

Once we were engaged in one of my favorite activities – hunting for a cow that was calving in the woods. Oh, what a wonderful feeling to pick up a wobbly calf in my arms and have the mother bellowingly follow me home! This time my hero-brother accidentally walked through a huge hornet nest. He didn't get stung at first – but I did! I stood there, paralyzed, and screamed. So did my brother. I can still hear him, "Run, you damn fool!" But no – he had to come back through the yellow jacket nest and carry <u>me</u> home instead of the calf that he hadn't located! We were two well-punctured human beings. I still sense the odor and texture of the muck they covered me in, to reduce the stingings.

I started first grade at five. It was in a one-room school that I was introduced to the wonderful world of color as in a new box of <u>six</u> Crayolas. I can still feel my reverence for those 6 crayons. I've always loved color whether in art, nature, or food.

The reading primer, "<u>See Dick and Jane</u>," opened great future adventures for me.

This is going to be hard to believe. There were ten grades taught to nineteen students in that room. I was the youngest that year and Red was among the oldest.

My Mom or Dad was always on the school board. They had contrived to get a qualified high school teacher so that they could educate the community children, mostly ours, until we were old enough to go away from home, work for our room and board, and graduate from high school. Our family, especially Red, always did well in school.

During the elementary school years, Roger had skipped a grade. He still graduated from 8$^{th}$ grade with the best achievement scores in Langlade County.

He was on stage for an honor award and fainted. Because of this,

Dad said he didn't think the kid had a brain in his head!

Roger never mentioned this. However, he did tell me recently he refused to go to school in his ninth year because he was so small. The other three in his class were big hulks!

Dad allowed him to stay home and work on the farm for a year. By then, he had grown enough to face his peers!

Roger went to Wabeno High School his senior year. He deliberately tried to keep his grades down so as not to be a valedictorian. He did not want to give a speech! As second highest in his class, he had to give a speech anyway!

On his 18th birthday, he was drafted into WWII.

My beloved brother Roger ("Red") just passed away this week, April 24, 2014. He would have been 89 at the end of May.

I've adored Roger all my life. Words cannot describe the void that he has left behind!

However, Roger's life has shone a light into this world that will always be remembered by those of us who knew him. Thanks, Red!

Red turned out best. He eventually earned a doctorate in Bio-Chemistry. He worked for four decades at the C.D.C. in Savannah and Atlanta, Georgia. Red was an invited speaker by the World Health Organization, a number of times, throughout the world. He read papers detailing his own work and discoveries or inventions. "Your mother's buttons popped many, many times over 'my son!"

Throughout the years, the good priest would stop and visit my Dad. They'd go lake fishing. Once, when I was nine, I was helping them catch minnows, Father said, "You know, you should become a fisher of men!" I didn't know what he was talking about at the time, but it did sound adventurous.

No one ever talked to me about God. Every Christmas we got to listen to a radio program called, "The Little One." It was the story of a donkey that carried Mary to Bethlehem; probably the same donkey that breathed on Baby Jesus to keep Him warm. I was captivated by the ring of the donkey's hooves on the cobblestones. That was the extent of my religion!

Until I was twelve, religion was a taboo subject.

Life to me had no meaning, no value whatsoever. Mom had tried hard to give her first six children a Protestant upbringing. Dad had tried just as hard to kill that movement.

Then came the "Brides of Christ" and the struggle for life, for both of us, when I was born. Mom was too tired and confused to sort it out. She reacted by saying "To hell with God – He's dead!" Certainly she felt that her own soul was so. She had no fight left in her at the time. Life was hard enough on her without trying to let God in, too.

The first six grew up searching. Their searches led them to different faiths. There were Greek Orthodox, Lutherans, Baptists, Methodists, and one inquiring Catholic.

## *Twelve*

### A SURPRISE VISIT

When I was five, my Grandma was dying. One of her sons called a priest and "Granny" got "squared away." Living in a world where it might be O.K. if you were seen occasionally but damn well never be heard, it's amazing that I left home and sneaked up to her house, where the grown-ups were.

One day, a wonderful priest was visiting her. All I recollect was a minor explosion from my parents, because I was supposed to have stayed home where I belonged.

Lo and behold, this man in beautiful black clothes put his arm around me and asked my name! That was up to then, in my memory, the most important moment of my life – in some ways, to this day, it still is. Someone paid attention to me. I existed! Isn't that wild?

When we'd go grocery shopping in the nearest town, if one was extremely lucky, one might once a year or so, come across some very mysterious and fascinating human beings, shopping in the Woolworth Dime Store. As I remember, these women, (or were they women?), were not too awfully happy to have me trail around the aisles with them. They always came in two's. They wore tantalizing long black and white dresses.

Well, at some time, after my pestering her to death, Mom

explained that they were Brides of Christ. Wow!

One spring day when I was twelve, I was eating a bowl of cereal after school. In came the familiar sound of Father's Model A. Now I mentioned that we saw this man probably at the extreme, about twice a year. But we lived far out in the wooded country. I hesitate to call it wilderness – yet, if I took a city person there today, I know that it would be perceived as wilderness even now. When a car went by, we could all describe it. If, an airplane wandered into our atmosphere, we all ran out to watch it. So I knew this was Father's car. Good God, and I was home alone? I hid my cereal bowl under my chair – certainly priests didn't eat. Later, as I stood talking to him, that bowl sat ludicrously planted under Dad's open chair!

I did my best to entertain Father, like my Dad would have. I took him upstairs to show him Mom's hundreds and hundreds of canned quarts of food. We had no other way to preserve food, so this was a source of pride. There were vegetables, fruit, berries, canned chicken, pork, beef, and venison, also rows of jellies and jams and home-made wines. I just remembered something really special. Mom canned homemade pork sausages. It was our only way to preserve them. This was our "Show and Tell!"

Knowing the above and knowing that for practical purposes I was an only child, as I grew up – you must realize, by now, who my "father's son" was, or the non-paid hired hand! Every piece of work that was ever done on a farm was my specialty. No baled hay or combined oats were moved without my help. Cows were milked by hand and my all-time specialty was shoveling manure, be it chicken, pig, horse or cow!

I never missed a day of school. I was not one to be fooled; -- it was a lot easier raising your hand to a teacher's question than manning a manure shovel.

As Father was leaving, he leaned out the window and said, "How would you like to go to summer school for three weeks in June? I'd arrange to have a neighbor transport you." Now Father certainly had to have spoken to my Dad about this previously.

As I remember, I had no idea that this involved religion. I'm sure Father had no idea that I didn't realize that. All I knew was that for three weeks, I'd get out of some hard work on the farm. I didn't know that it would involve those mysterious "Brides of Christ." Of course, I'd like to go to summer school!

## Thirteen

## THERE IS ANOTHER WORLD!

Now, years later, this thought struck me for the first time. I wonder if that meeting was staged? Perhaps Dad had arranged for both Mom and he to be away when Father came. Certainly, I remember no discussion with anyone about my attending catechism. The neighbor who took me to class, along with his children, must have gone without pay, twenty miles out of his way, twice a day, to transport me.

I was mesmerized by the goodness, gentility and holiness in those nuns. In the Solemn Communion Class, Sister gave me a collection of Junior Scholastics that her students had used the previous year. Every word in those weekly papers soaked into my dry soul like water into desert soil.

I am blessed with a good intellect and photogenic memory of life experiences. During those three weeks of catechism, my hand was up to answer every question. It became a frustration for Sister. She tried not to make an issue of it, but at times my hand was the only one raised. She burst her cool when the question was, "What is Pope Pius X remembered for?" No one had the slightest inkling. She was forced by circumstances to call on me – "Of course, I know, Sister! He let little children receive Holy Communion!"

I've always wished that I could have heard what she said. She went on and on and on, and some of it must have been good! I mean, I'm sure she was saying some nice things about me, but I was so embarrassed that I couldn't hear!

Because my brother was in the Army, some agency had once sent him a bronze dog tag. That bronze looked like gold to me! On it was printed the "Our Father." Well, I stole the tag and memorized the "Our Father." So when Sister wanted to know if I knew any prayers, I was real proud to recite my stolen "Our Father!" As I finished my rendition, "For thine is the Power and the Glory Forever and ever. Amen." she quietly said, "We don't say that part!" Did I join the Church, or did the Church join me? I seem to recall saying it in Church all the time now! Isn't that funny?

On June 21, 1947 I was baptized by Father at our Catholic parish. The next day I received my First Holy Communion along with the large Solemn Communion group of children my age. Nothing in my life has ever affected me more.

Everything about my life changed. Life had meaning and value for the first time. I quit stealing; I quit lying! Would wonders never cease?

Six weeks later I asked Dad to take me to the church early so that I could go to Confession. His answer was, "Whatever for? You don't say damn anymore and you say, 'Excuse me' when you walk in front of the horses!"

In those days one fasted from food and water from midnight in order to receive Communion. We attended 10:00 a.m. Mass. No one went to Communion. Well, I did! For at least a year, people would encourage me to leave my pew or say, "Now!" But I'd freeze; I couldn't get up and walk alone up to the altar. What if I'd make a mistake? So after Mass, Father would come down and give me Holy Communion.

Six months later, my mother began to take instructions. The only time that I ever saw a sign of affection between my parents was the day Mom told Dad that she wanted to become a Catholic. He folded her in his arms and kissed her – in front of me!

In my home, pride and intelligence were prized commodities. Basically, any visible emotions and signs of affection among adults were taboo.

My father accompanied my mother to her instructions. Dad was not well and he fell asleep during a lot of those sessions. Father thought that Dad was a fallen-away Catholic coming back to the Church. Actually, Dad knew nothing about the Faith and never was, and never did, become a Catholic. He just wanted a little peace of soul – maybe like to go to Church on Christmas and Easter. That kind of stuff.

Mom reconnected with her God and proceeded forward into a full-blown love affair with God and His Church.

So unsuspectingly, Dad had moved his checkers into squares on his checkerboard of life, where he was to be jumped again and again. In the end, God won the game and I'm sure He enveloped my father in Eternal Peace. But for my Dad, the game of life was hell!

Mom and Dad were baptized conditionally because their previous records were unavailable. Dad received his First Holy Communion on June 16, 1948. Poor Mom tied a red handkerchief around the pump in the kitchen sink so as not to break her fast. She was on her way, out of the house, to go to church, -- when she turned back, absent-mindedly untied the kerchief, and drank some water! Mom made her Communion the following week. Once – a green pea, and another time, -- a wild strawberry – beat us out of Communion!

## Fourteen

## I HAVE A DREAM!

So now, we're back to June, 1948. A year had passed and I was again attending Catechism. I had just graduated from eighth grade. Within me burst a new ideal! I wanted to become a Bride of Christ. So I told Father, "I want to be a nun!" I'm sure I blew his mind! He was known for being a terrible tease. Father's witty retort was "Oh, you want to become a 'nothing', is that it?"

In some ways, you know, that is the very essence of Religious Life. I've spent my entire life since that day trying to become less, in order that there may be more of Christ in me. Sometimes, I've shouted the prayer out loud. I've written it or whispered it softly so that perhaps God wouldn't hear. As the years have flown by, I've sometimes hidden so that God didn't get any more crazy ideas about emptying me more. I've shielded my face and yelled, "Enough of this, God!"

I guarantee you that this is a prayer God will always answer! Heaven jumps for joy, if you ask God to empty you of yourself in order to make more room for Him.

I've mentioned how authoritarian both of my parents were. I was basically, as far as I was concerned, an only child. My father was forty-four and my mother thirty-six, when I was born. By the time I finished eighth grade, Mom was forty-nine and Dad was fifty-seven.

I do not ever remember my parents telling me "No" for anything that I ever requested. Now mind you, I was <u>extremely</u> cautious about anything I ever asked for! I was sure I would get it or I certainly wouldn't ask. I was proud and "No" was simply a word I could not handle. And <u>I</u> was going to take a vow of Obedience?

I never asked Dad to let me go to the Convent. I had never crossed him in my life. But now there was a Greater Force directing me. Apparently, Father talked to my parents and told them of my desire.

I know that Dad was afraid to have me attend a public high school. Many bad things went on fifty years ago – believe it or not. There were stories of "naked, non-virgin, <u>snake</u> dances!" in town at night. There was a U.S. Air Force base located not too far away. Marijuana and cocaine and pregnancies were rampant.

I had received a list of clothing items needed for the convent. Mom and I were shopping just before school was to open. As he was about to drive away, Dad asked, "Do you have everything for school?"

Mom said, "Yes, but I didn't get stockings. I didn't know what color to get."

Dad said, "Damn it! Get her black!"

So dear Bishop, that was my Father's tacit approval; his <u>only</u> approval given me, for all the years that I was in the convent.

# *Fifteen*

## A NEW WORLD

To make this story really fun, you must understand that I had never stayed away from home overnight in my life. My father was too protective.

Before I knew it, I was knocking on the Convent door. My hair was still in braids and I really didn't know how to fix it myself! I was 100 miles from home. Our incoming and outgoing mail was read by our Superior. I had company once during the year. Us young girls, or Aspirants, did go home for the holidays. Other than that, I never left the Convent grounds.

How anyone – and everyone – myself included, allowed this to happen, I'll never understand. As naive as it was, if I were living my life over, <u>knowing all that I now know</u>, I would do the same thing again, all fourteen years of my convent experience. I also would leave again, when and as I did before!

It was 1948; I had been "sort of a Catholic" for fourteen months. As I look back, I had probably attended Mass less than thirty times tops, I had no idea who <u>I</u> really was; much less what made those nuns tick. Yet there was something exhilaratingly wonderful about it all when I could quit crying of homesickness. For once in my life, I was thin. I lost thirty pounds because of home sickness. I lost my appetite --)! Actually, part of that weight was hair! For survival's sake, the nuns talked me into cutting it!

I was a good student so I fit in there. They laughed at me in the laundry room. I was certainly never allowed to touch anything but hankies, -- and the laundress Sister used to make me do those over! I could have handled an ax but not a flat iron! I had not been taught any household skills. All my life, I had worked outside with my Dad.

The thing that I loved the most about that year was the practice and love of poverty that was so apparent.

I was used to great farm breakfasts. That first morning I was stunned. I had never seen cold cereal and apparently the nuns had never seen sugar! I truly thought I'd never survive those breakfasts – certainly not that first one! Many meals were accompanied by silence. I had come several days late and missed some explanations. I didn't know that we were not to talk until the Superior did. A third of the meal went by and no one spoke. I exclaimed, "Will someone say something before I go crazy?" Everyone laughed and Sister Bertilla gave us permission to talk.

There was the famous greyhouse. It was a six-stall outhouse. Toilet paper consisted of carefully-cut squares of newspaper. At least, there were no inane arguments about whether the paper should coil over or under the roll! After night prayers, during a time called "Grand Silence," all the nuns went down to the greyhouse. Only if you were ill or disabled or it was the middle of the night was anyone allowed to use the indoor facilities. Saving water was considered keeping the vow of poverty. Silence was kept throughout the night until after breakfast.

One winter night, while waiting in line for my turn, I witnessed one of the scariest, most beautiful sights of my entire life.

The sky was graced with a totally incomparable aurora borealis. Webster's dictionary defines this as "an electrical phenomenon consisting of streamers, bands, curtains, arcs, etc. of light, ordinarily confined to high or polar altitudes." It was all of that, and more. It was a theatrical spectacle.

It reminded me of drapes of old-fashioned hard Christmas candy, hanging above me. The night sky was predominantly red but contained vivid hues of every color of the rainbow. All this was powerfully undulating across the entire heavens. It mesmerized me into cold, shocking attention. I was sure that the world was about to end. I have never seen northern lights like that since.

The old laundry house was from another world. Clothes were washed each Monday and hung outside. If it was winter and they froze on the line, they were taken in and draped over the hot water, cast iron registers to dry. The laundry sported a huge wood-burning stove. If we were lucky, baked apples would be ready mid-morning for a treat. On top of this huge stove were probably fifty to eighty metal flat irons. You would use one until it got too cold and then release your wooden handle in order to transfer it to another hot iron. Unless you were there, you couldn't imagine the absolutely unique smell of that laundry. There were always about eighteen of us ironing. Some Sisters had the dubious honor of getting up at 3:00 a.m. and washing the clothes or starting a good fire in the stove.

One spring morning some fun loving smelt fishermen had left seven huge hundred-pound bags of smelt at the kitchen door. Twenty-two of us spent an entire day cleaning those little fish. I don't remember eating them, but I'll never forget cleaning them!

The nuns had this huge garden. They raised and canned their own food. They even had a barn, cows, geese, pigs and chickens. Now this was where I fit. When the laundress couldn't stand me anymore, she'd ship me off to the gardener. I truly loved this. Later, when I left for several years, it was the nun's love of Poverty that dauntingly drew me back.

This might sound like pride but that is not the reason for relating the next incident. I was still thirteen when we were administered a nationally standardized test, determining how much religious knowledge we vocational candidates had. Twenty-two of us, from ages thirteen to thirty-five, took the test. I had the second highest score. I missed one out of 100 questions. This question was a "yes or no" answer type. "You can offer a Mass to St. Anthony, in honor of Jesus, for a favor." The correct answer was "No." I had decided, "Yes," Wrong!

The Mass is offered in, through and with Jesus Christ. It is the re-enactment of the Holy Sacrifice on the cross.

Here's my point and it haunted me for many years – somewhat even yet today. My knowledge was head knowledge. I lacked the heart knowledge that comes from a normal, stable Catholic family. Knowledge and character do not necessarily mesh. I could never figure out those nuns. They all seemed to be better than myself and I did not know how to solve the dilemma!

At the end of that school year, the aspirants, (us little girls), went home for the summer. The next year it was decided to end the aspirancy – meaning those under sixteen. I had the opportunity to come back but I would have been the only one not old enough to become a postulant. It was finally decided that I should go home, grow up, and make my father, who had become very bitter about my being gone, a little less unhappy. I was welcome to come back the following year.

Five Aspirants in 1948-49. I am in the back row.
This is at the old convent at Bay Settlement. The building has been demolished.
This was the answer to Dad's "Damn it, get her black!" I was 14 years old.

# Sixteen

## BACK TO DISCORD

So this fourteen-year old went home to take on the big, bad world of public high school. Can you believe it? The nuns were sending me into a den of iniquity!

I liked my three years at Antigo High School, but I couldn't participate in sports or extracurricular activities because of long bus rides to and from school. These rides were the result of school districts consolidating. I had to be on the bus at 6 a.m. We arrived at 8 a.m. After school, I was on the bus at 4 p.m. and home at 6 p.m. I almost always had my homework done on the bus. Those two hour trips were 72 miles one way!

Arriving home that late, eating and living without electricity didn't allow for much activity. I read, listened to the news with my parents and was in bed at 9 p.m. The bus would be back at 6 a.m. With this schedule, I only did outside chores at home on weekends.

I stayed home four years. I didn't get to attend Mass regularly, perhaps only once every six to eight weeks. We were, after all, a total of fifteen miles from church. Neither Mom nor I had learned to drive. Dad would have had to teach us. At the time all cars were stick shifts. Everyone knew that Dad lacked the patience to teach anyone anything. Dad was pretty well convinced that he wasn't going to take us to church very damn often. It suffices to say that the Protestant/Catholic Irish war between my parents was still subtly fought on a daily – certainly nightly – basis.

There were many nights that I pulled the covers over my head to blot out the fight that <u>now</u> at least always ended in myself and the Convent and who was to blame! I am not exaggerating when I say that I seriously worried that Dad might choke my mother some night just to shut her up. He would start the fights but she would never let them die. I adored my dad, bastard that he was. I began to hate my mother for the saint that she was. I could never understand how Dad could always be wrong and Mom was always right and yet that's the way it was about everything. I don't mean that Mom thought she was always right. In every move of her life, I still believe she was always right and God, how I hated her for it!

Battles started with events that were years old. One famous oft repeated battle started with, "I picked all those berries and you threw them out!"

It was a hot summer day. She had five children to care for and she 'was' probably pregnant.

I not only would have thrown them out, I probably would have stomped on them!

Her only fault was that she wouldn't shut up. "Just shut up, Ma, before I choke you myself," seemed to be my own national anthem.

Now I must explain I personally cannot, will not fight, unless I am backed into a corner and its fight, escape, or die. Either I am innately wise or a terrible coward.

Later in life, Mom and I discussed this. Her explanation was beautifully powerful and clear. She was fighting for survival. Dad and the circumstances in her life had caused her to lose faith in her God for years and she would under no condition let it happen again.

Coward that I was – I never got involved in any of those fights. I pussyfooted around Dad's anger.

I have a great uncanny way of knowing who's hurting even in a happy crowd. Those who hurt intuitively know that and take advantage of the solace they find in me. I often feel that I could reach into and hold anyone's emotional pain long enough for them to catch their breath, to get the strength to continue on with their own burden. I know that I can do this boldly, invasively, and do it without causing further pain. This gift was developed during those painful years at home.

One time I was away from home for some reason. My brother drove me into the yard – a good distance from the house. I remember saying, "I can't go in. They're fighting."

He said, "How can you possibly know?"

I answered, "Let me tell you, I know!" I feel it. It proved to be true.

To this day, I know when there's tension regardless of who it involves. It produces grating discords in the Song of Life.

It has followed me into married life. My husband will attest to this, I am sure. I read the language of doors slamming, heavy footsteps, silverware banging, etc. It _all_ agitates me.

On the other hand, my husband is rather quiet. But if he can't find a nail, or stumbles over something in the basement or God forbid the kids didn't put something away correctly – which by the way they often don't – I hear this loud voice coming from him. We may not have had a need to speak to each other for hours but suddenly he's talking to himself or banging something around loud enough just for my benefit – just to make his point. Now after dancing around my father, in a boxing stance for years, the sound of this masculine game infuriates the hell out of me! Once again, I could cheerfully choke a neck! Guess whose?

Under this I wore the first store-bought dress I ever had. It was a gift from Roger.

## Seventeen

## WE CARRY OUR OWN BAGGAGE

We each carry our own childhood baggage with us. The baggage Dad saddled me with as a child has followed me every moment of my life. It was greatly responsible for my inability to smoothly adapt to many convent situations.

Had I, at the time, been out in the work-a-day, lay world, I would have experienced the same problems. We all have to deal with authority. There has to be order in the world. For that to happen, we have to give and take. Some people are in leadership positions. In order to lead, there must be people who are subjective enough to be intelligent followers.

This is an essential issue of Church Unity today. There must be authority and obedience or at least co-operative teamwork. Both public and Catholic schools are far from perfect. We all rebel against authority.

But when students with only a Catholic education knock heads with nuns in an educational system, or adults clash with priests, they aim their emotional antipathy toward the Church and God.

Christian authority at its <u>ideal</u> is still <u>authority</u>. Youth resents <u>any</u> authority. People, of any age who haven't matured, still resent authority.

We need to realize that all normal life involves authority and not forever blame the Church for the stupid mistakes of some priest or nun.

But people continually do this. We all hear it repeatedly.

I don't go to Church because Fr. So-and-so did such-and-such, years ago. To those people I wish I had the guts to say, "Grow up! Are you going to be an adolescent forever?"

This in no way refers to the sexual scandal involving some priests. There is absolutely unequivocally, no excuse for that!

Deep down inside all of us who are festering and brooding, we know that it's great comforting fun to lick our wounds. We also know that growing up involves real pain and it's easier to just stagnate in emotional childhood.

I graduated from high school. How could I leave home? I didn't know what I wanted to do with my life. If I left, Dad might kill Ma. He really wanted to possess my life as well as Mom's. He also needed my physical labor on the farm.

I must state that these fights were all verbal and emotional. Never, ever, would my father have angrily touched my mother. He maybe never even thought of choking her. That may only have been my fantasy!

I do know something that I've never told anyone before. One day, as I passed the garage, having finished the farm work, I noticed that the car was running and the fumes were pouring out under the tightly closed doors. I hesitated, knowing what was going on, as to whether I dared cross my father enough to question what the hell he thought he was doing. When I opened the garage door to politely ask him if he realized that he had the car running with the garage doors closed, the shock of being caught clearly stood out in his eyes. There was no doubt whatsoever that he was attempting suicide. This was never again mentioned between us. But you better bet I kept an eye out for suspicious behavior from then on!

By now, I had come to a full realization that although I loved those "Brides of Christ," I really didn't want to be one! The mystery was gone. I even knew how they got dressed! That always used to bug me before I entered the convent.

I loved poverty. I loved chastity but that obedience thing was just not my cup of tea.

The only reason that I went to the Convent in the first place was a great, open-hearted response to God's gift of Baptism. My life had gone from absolutely no meaning to a full embrace of the Great Being. I wanted to return to Him what He had given to me.

If someone gives you a lovely gift – wholeheartedly – you desire to reciprocate. All my life, I've wanted to give back to God, what He gave to me in Baptism.

Through all my 80 years, I have not been famous for always showing up when I'm supposed to be in church. My heart might yearn to attend but my mind or body might not be able to co-operate. I have crippling arthritis and am fatigued and overweight; I can just demand so much out of this body that St. Francis called, "Brother Ass!" However, I have been blessed to live almost every moment of my life, knowing that I walk and talk with God. He has always held my hand and I am sure that if I someday look back on the sands of time, it will be really clear, by the pattern of the footprints on the path, when the Lord carried me!

# Eighteen

## THE GREEN LIGHT AND SULPHURIC SMELL OF LIGHTNING

One morning when I was eighteen, I decided enough was enough. Dad couldn't claim me forever. I would run away, borrow money, and go to my brother, Red, who lived in St. Louis. Dawn had followed a night of particular bad squabbling which was still going on. It was a hot, muggy morning. I went to get the cows down in the south-forty. For some reason, I lay face down on the ground among the hazel bushes that were loaded with nuts. I prayed as I had never prayed before.

I had finally arrived upon a solution to this war mess – God was to take me – no matter how – sickness, car accident, lightning; whatever – I especially mentioned lightning. If I died, my parents would surely feel so bad, they'd quit fighting! My sister later told me that my parents always fought when the other siblings were growing up. I didn't know that. To my awareness and at least at this time in their life, the fighting seemed always to be about me.

I went home and packed all my belongings in a box, leaving my parents a note to send these things to Red. I also succinctly informed them that having watched their great marital bliss, I would never be caught dead in that state of life!

I intended to wait till Dad was busily distracted and then I was going to go to a neighbor's on my bike in order to get help to go away.

Those hazel nuts were a prime crop. I couldn't leave Dad without a sign of love so I went back to the forty and picked a huge burlap bag full of nuts for him. By now, I really "hated" Ma and she would just have to adjust to my not having a good-bye gift for her!

I came onto the porch with my sack full of nuts. It was eerily hot and muggy.

Dad said, "Hey, girl, let's beat the storm and get the cows. "I'll drive you around to the south forty."

As I was bringing the cows home, I knew that I was in a very dangerous situation.

The lightning began, with air that was heavy green and sulphur-like. On one side of me was a barbed wire fence. Ahead of me was a woods and I knew I couldn't go by either one. So I went in between. The cows by now were moving far ahead. I smelled the lightning. I didn't see or hear it. As I was passing under a lone basswood tree between the fence and the woods, the bolt struck.

When I came to, I was lying over a stump and the dog was licking my face.

I thought I remembered following the fence line. Every time I came to the barbs on the wire that I thought were dripping with flames, I lifted my hand!

Seeing that my whip was found in an entirely different direction, it tells me that my mind was playing tricks. I wasn't near the fence.

I don't think that I imagined the next story. I came to the river and tried to run across as though it was a level road. I landed ker-splat belly down in the water.

I thought when I got to where the river came to our pasture that I faced a big beautiful red barn. No such barn existed for miles nor was I anywhere near home.

Dad carried me home and as the two of them were taking me to the car and racing me to the hospital – guess what? They were still fighting – about me!

That was my first episode of trying to tell God how to do things.

If there's anything to the present day theory of energy fields within or surrounding us, I'd like to posit the theory that those get scrambled during a lightning strike. It's as if the electrodes in your brain get jumbled.

Dad caught up with me, racing blindly through a cedar swamp, completely in the opposite direction from home.

He said every time it lightened during his trying to guide me home, I turned thunderstruck and screamed toward the direction of the strike.

I remained in the hospital four days (Today, they would have "treated and released" me.) Because I had rubber-soled boots the lightning grounded and didn't damage me or burn me. It just "fried" my brain a little!

Mom and Dad came to visit me in the hospital carrying splinters from an inch long to five feet. The tree had burst into literal toothpicks.

When I was sleeping at the hospital, if something noisy like a food cart would go by I'd wake up screaming.

Several weeks later, I wanted to enroll in a nearby Teachers' Normal School. Dad was giving his usual, "I need you on the farm bit," when Mom helped me escape by saying, "For God's sake, Frank, you almost lost her for good, two weeks ago!"

Later when I was teaching, I'd always pull the classroom drapes and turn on the lights if it was storming. My explanation?

"You can watch storms when you're home. Here you look out the window and get distracted!" The kids bought that! They never guessed that it was I who would have been crazily, cowardly distracted.

Some of my classmates who attended the same college I did, years later, surely must remember what a circus I was during one thunder storm.

A group of us slept in metal cots. That summer, mine happened to be headed toward a wall against a metal radiator.

There was one ferocious storm on a hot, muggy night. Flashes of light were splattering all over the black playground outside. My naïve dorm mates wouldn't shut the windows because it was too hot inside and the rain obviously wasn't coming in the windows!

I spent much of that night, grown nun that I was, sobbingly crunched up in a ball in my nightgown and robe in the corner of the school hall where I couldn't see the lightning.

# *Nineteen*

## RE-ENTERING THE CONVENT

Another year passed and God's waiting. I told Him that I didn't want to go back to the Convent. Love the Nuns? Yes! Join them? No!

Eventually I sent in my application. I still had that echo within me that I couldn't drown out. "Give back to God what He gave to you!" No human ever gave me that idea. God Himself was to blame for that! In God's checker game, it was time now for <u>my</u> move.

August came. I had moved to St. Louis to stay with my brother and sister-in-law for three months. I was working in a huge department store, Stix-Baer & Fuller. I couldn't foresee a future there; I felt my brother and sister-in-law must surely want me to leave. My sister-in-law knew that I had sent in my application but I obviously was making no move to get ready to leave. So she asked me what I was going to do. It was about a week before entrance day. I distinctly remember thinking – "Oh, what the hell, I'll go back!"

Wasn't that a great motivating thrust toward answering the call of God?

In the year that I had worked after high school, I had saved enough money for my hundred-dollar dowry. As I remember, this was not to be spent by the religious community as long as I lived.

I'm sure it must have been invested but the principal stayed in my name in case I would ever choose to leave. It was sort of a "nest egg." That was the policy of the religious communities at that time.

I had a small footlocker filled with all the personal toiletries and clothing that I thought I would need during the next three years during which I needed to pay my own personal expenses. I also possessed three hundred dollars extra for unexpected needs that might come up.

I had to be self-sufficient. Certainly there was no one else whom I could rely upon in case of necessity. I was well prepared.

Three nights before I was to leave home, a sister of a dear friend of mine, told me that she wanted to become a nun, had to leave home for security reasons also. Her father molested her sisters.

She simply couldn't <u>afford</u> to enter. She had no money and was dirt-poor. Just sixteen years of age, she had no way to finance herself.

I wrote to the Mother Superior of the convent I had chosen and persuaded her in understanding that two vocations were better than one. So this sixteen-year old was allowed to enter without a dowry. I paid my dowry, divided every personal item in my trunk in half so the "other" half was Anna's! Thus, Father presented two girls for entrance into the Community on that memorable Sunday afternoon.

Anna was scared silly. My dad had just loudly and clearly disowned me. My guiding priest "Father Hubert," was a terrible tease. So when one of the nuns in charge of the postulants, (who later became a life-long mental adversary of mine), answered the door, Father said, "Sister, I am bringing you a future Mother Superior!" I giggled and was from then on labeled an emotional, highly intelligent nincompoop! (Those words, by the way, are not my own.) Every nun who ever reads this will want to laugh, nod their head, or cry, but they will fully understand, because in those days, that was foreseen as the way to make you humble, or as Father had earlier remarked, "become a nothing!"

I still contend that life itself humbles you and that the kind of humility gained by life experiences is sincere. The other approach, I think, builds false humility. I personally am living proof that it can breed intense anger that became stored in my soul and festered like hell.

I have loved Religious Life for fifty years. I have loved those "Brides of Christ" for over sixty years.

I have also let crap like the above, store and rot and ulcerate until it choked the life air out of me. Much of my interior life has been like the bronchial burn that I am now struggling against. This is by far not the first time I have choked and gulped and struggled for the air that sustains life. I have often felt like the fish in a polluted tank gasping for oxygen. This has been my struggle for survival since the day my mother finally decided to quit dying and push me out of her womb.

Taken in 1953 – the day I left home for the Convent.

# *Twenty*

## A DEVOTION THAT ABSORBED MY LIFE

    *I* have no intention of dragging anyone chronologically through any of these years. I shall write what the Holy Spirit says needs to be written and only once more, I state my right to ramble.

So the first year of my new convent adventure was spent in what was called at the time, a Pre-Novitiate. It was at the Chapel at Robinsonville, WI. In front of a lovely statue of the Blessed Virgin Mary, I privately dedicated my life to her in what was entitled the St. Louis de Montfort devotion. I did not have the Superior's permission for this nor did I ask for it. She'd surely have said, "No," had I asked for it. She would have said "No," just to say, "No." And as I have already indicated, "No" is a word that I had a terrible time accepting! It is true, this devotion has caused both great consternation and confusion and finally, great peace in my life. Essentially as I interpret it, it says, "I am nothing!"

Now I know that in the long run – we all are nothing. God has certainly taught me that often, or I have concluded that, often while wrestling with Him, in my on-going checkerboard game.

The devotion consists of seeing oneself as nothing. It involves giving oneself and all that one has – merits, value, rights to the Blessed Mother for life and Eternity. She, because of her closeness to God while on earth and now as Queen of Heaven, embellishes the gift of nothingness that we offer. Therefore, as a glowing golden gift, our nothingness is offered by her to God, through Christ.

What perhaps is, was, or might have been – any value or reward we were having, or was to come, was freely given to Christ. This was to be used wherever it was most needed for sinners, or wherever the need was greatest. Now, that is *my* understanding. Therefore, the devotee meets God in Eternity totally poverty-stricken or naked, relying completely upon the Eternal Mercy of One's Creator.

Now my life-long problem with this is that I'm not really sure if there is any reality to it. I mean, I've learned nothing is mine to count on anyway. Everything is gift. Nothing ever really was mine and so maybe I have nothing to give to begin with. At any rate, to this day, I can get caught up in mental anguish wrestling with this non-ending circle!

I do believe that when I return to my maker, my loved one, that He will open wide His arms to receive and embellish my nothingness.

Yesterday, April 27, 2014, two great popes were declared saints. Both of them lived in my lifetime. They were Pope John XXIII, who wisely called the Vatican Counsel. He saw that the church needed new light and air.

Pope John Paul II, who came from Poland, was the first non-Italian pope in over 800 years.

Pope John Paul II made the same St. Louis de Montfort consecration in his life that I've spoken of.

John Paul II suffered terribly from Parkinson's disease. He did not resign because he was extremely mentally alert and able to carry out his duties.

He wanted to show the sick and elderly that there was dignity in their life.

Knowing about him has certainly given dignity to my life. I hope the world recognizes what he has given us!

# Twenty-One

## AT LAST – A BRIDE OF CHRIST

Finally, Reception Day did come – that wonderful day in every nun's life when she receives the religious habit and a new name and identity.

A Mennonite minister's wife, married to Dad's cousin, coerced my father into coming to my Reception. She was visiting my parents and wanted to experience the ceremony. Now my mother always totally supported anything I did – even when I left the convent! (Actually, that could have killed her, but she went with the flow.)

I want the world to know that my father adored me. He hated my being a nun with a passion because it was something he couldn't control. On the other hand, he was always proud of his nun daughter so much that he could have burst, according to what his farmer friends said. The great problem was he just couldn't make any sense out of it. He was basically a control freak and this whole thing was well beyond his own power.

The Reception ceremony was mind-bending. When my hair was cut, I was so filled with that sense of nothingness that I could taste it.

There were ten of us in our class. We entered the church dressed as Brides. I had finally reached that goal!

We received our habits and went down in the church basement

where our hair was cut. Women have always considered hair their crown of glory. Symbolic of humility our heads were covered with veils.

We came up from the basement dressed as nuns, only as novices, we wore white veils.

I was given my first choice of names, Sister Maureen. I was now a Sister and my heart <u>sang</u> like Mary in her Magnificat. Maureen, in Ireland, meant "little Mary".

Mary became as nothing to be the handmaid of the Lord. Through her emptiness she made room for the Holy Spirit to overshadow her, and the Incarnate Word of God became Man. I firmly believe that we each have the power through the Holy Spirit, to give birth to Jesus Christ in the stable of our lives, every moment that we breathe!

We all have shepherds in our lives that come and see the Babe born in our stable. The Father sends a star to guide the Wise Men to our door. Heavenly hosts of angels sing "Alleluia!" I know; I know; I know they do! I have heard them symbolically all my life!

It's just that sometimes we allow the personal crap in our life to pile up, so high that it hides our own "pony."

I have cried – maybe twenty times in my life. Tears were frozen into a Titanic glacier and I've thought for sure they would never melt again.

While writing the above, I broke into tears. I knew if the prophecy ever came true, there would be a virtual El Nino.

My husband just woke up to hear me sobbing. Knowing how ill I've been, he thought I couldn't breathe again. I assured him that the wrenching sobbing was just God's rain washing a muddy, mildewy, purulent landscape fresh and clean and that the air was free of contamination for once!

Dear God, thank you for the gift of tears and thank you for letting me cry in front of my family. I was free and not walled and hidden! Thank you even more that I am aware of why I'm crying. It's hell to cry, and cry, and cry – and not know why. Years ago, that contributed to my leaving the Convent.

One of my sons was going to work during my crying jag. He has probably never seen me cry. He just said, "Have a good day, Mom!" He and I are much alike. We sometimes bedevil the hell out of each other. Little does he know that these tears and this book are the harbinger of The Great New Day of the rest of my life, for however long God wishes to extend it. Whatever the duration, whatever the pain or joy that lies ahead, I know that it will blend into the final, everlasting day of Eternal Life and laughter, at the Eternal Party, to which we have all been invited.

As a postulant 1953-54

Reception Day Aug. 12, 1954

Cousins Emily and Carol on Reception Day.

## Twenty-Two

## CHRISTMAS IN MY LIFE

For my own peace of mind, I must go back to the dowry, etc. This caused great pain and even after all these years that infected carbuncle must be lanced and the poison set free. As the Doctor said about the carbuncle on the base of my head, when I was a baby, "There is enough poison in there to kill a grown man!"

My friend, Anna, who entered the convent with me, was young, attractive and clever. Everyone loved her. That was more than fine. I loved her also and always will, although I haven't heard from her in forty years. She left the convent long before I did.

The hurt came when her parents, who were poor but much less poor than mine, visited frequently, giving her moral, social and monetary support.

I had divided all my possessions and money with her and I had very little money left for my own needs. No one really knew this. Anna didn't – and the Convent authorities did not understand this and for God's sake, I was too proud to tell them or ask for help! I was terribly short of underclothing – wearable stockings, nightgowns, etc. The Sisters knew that Anna was poor and they saw to it that she got what she needed if her family didn't provide it. One Christmas she was given a Care package.

Christmas in my life up to then was always sad and hurtful. We had nothing basically with which to decorate a tree. Having no electricity, we had none of those beautiful lights that other people had. Our old tree balls might today be expensive antiques but they were ugly in my sight.

We'd hunt for hours for the prettiest tree that we could find. One year Red and I found a tree that was almost totally covered with cones. It was probably a black swamp spruce that lost its needles in a week, but to this day it's still the prettiest tree I've ever seen. I used the branches that we needed to trim off the tree for bouquets. I'll never forget how pretty those cones were.

Any Christmas present that I ever received was home-made. If I hadn't seen Mom make it, I had definitely snooped until there was no surprise left. After having received so many nightgowns, mittens, and socks over the years, it was hard to muster any joy.

Well, this year in the Convent, I needed a nightgown. They gave Anna one that she didn't even need! Isn't life funny? Sometimes, aren't funny things cruel?

This will become quite a story by itself. In the convent, it was "all those other people" who got to decorate the Christmas tree. By that I mean, "anyone, except 'poor me'!" as I was usually cooking or baking.

The veil received on Reception Day. Sr. Maureen and Sr. Priscilla – Anna and me.

## Twenty-Three

## THE JOY OF HOLIDAYS

    *I* would decorate the classroom, along with my students' help, to my heart's content. However, there was still that painful spot in my heart called, "The others got to decorate the tree!" Actually, some of them probably wished they were doing something else! Maybe they wanted to cook!

This is for my beloved husband and sons. Now you know why Christmas in our home has been heavenly, magical; (Now you know why "Ma" always decorated the tree by herself). I remember, if you don't, husband, hugging you on those first Christmas mornings and thanking you for letting me truly have Christmas. I never had a Christmas, before I had it in our house with you. Now you know why you probably always felt like a heel at holiday times. I did so much that I'm sure I made you feel guilty for just contributing what any normal human being would do.

I know that our sons must look back upon their childhood and realize that, comparatively speaking they were raised poor. Part of that was very deliberate. Holy Poverty, as in the vow, is a wonderfully liberating possession. I know from my own childhood that material poverty is not the end of the world.

I have a real hard time justifying charity drives. I <u>know</u> poverty; I respect it. Material things and even a wealth of food will never fill a starving soul. We are much more resilient than we think. Poverty itself does not stunt the growth of the soul.

I fail to understand how any mentally healthy, able-bodied adults in this country cannot at least partially support themselves.

I totally cannot comprehend any parent, be it man or woman, who cannot save enough in 365 days of the year to make their own Christmas. People may have to give up alcohol, cigarettes, gambling and drugs. That money will make Christmas come. It arrives every year. It's not like it's a surprise event.

My brother said the year he received two presents, that he knew that we were rich. Both presents were jackknives!

In my married life, Christmas and Easter were both magic. The house was always decorated to the highest level of perfection that I could achieve. We always had a beautiful tree. It usually came from our wooded lot at the cottage, having originally been planted by us from sapling or seed!

Our house turned into a bakery at holiday time. Almost everything that the "rich kids" had in their homes year around, our kids were given as presents at Christmas or Easter. They received toys, skates, skis, sporting equipment, stereo, microwave, large T.V., pool table, pinball machine, electric dart board, Nintendo, water beds, bows and arrows, guns, and this last year, top of the line vacuum cleaners for their next step in life. My sons are now in their 40's.

On Easter we always had the best of Polish foods. We would fill a huge basket of all our specialties. My husband and sons would take the basket of food and wine to the altar at the local parish on Holy Saturday. The steps around the altar would be lined with colorful aromatic baskets of food. The priest would bless all the baskets with holy water.

On Easter Sunday morning after Mass, the house would be full of relatives eating the blessed food at breakfast.

One time I was ill and the next week was one of the boy's First

Communion celebrations. I said to my oldest son, "I don't have to make a big deal out of Easter, this year, do I?"

He said, "Oh, Mom, Easter is almost better in our house than Christmas!"

So I dug in to make another memorable Easter for my kids. Over the years they had received Big Wheels, bicycles, huge salamanders, homemade buddy dolls, and teddy bears, Packer equipment and Packer umbrellas on Easter morning.

The reason "Easter was almost better than Christmas in our house," was because their "rich" friends just got candy! Our sons got to celebrate the New Life of Easter in a unique way.

Now as Paul Harvey would say, "You know the rest of the story!

My sister, Helen, her daughter, Carol, and me. Helen is already wearing my clothes!

School Pictures of Sister Maureen

1958

1961

# Twenty-Four

## THE HILARITY OF LOOKING BACK AT REALITY

My third year in the convent, as a second year Novice, I was sent out to teach. Five of us from our class of ten were sent out a year early. We were promised our year of education later.

I loved teaching. If I could have closed my classroom door so that no "nun" would have seen or heard my mistakes, I could have foreseen teaching for all eternity, and considered it Heaven.

I loved the kids and they loved me. Neither of us had to hide. They could be themselves. Somehow their nutty teacher loved each of them. For me, children were never a threat. They hadn't yet learned to play the adult games of subterfuge.

One of my Sister companions on that first mission in Darboy is doing a beautiful job of typing my manuscript. It's been forty-three years since we were together but the night that I was so inundated with the need to write this story, I was also strongly impelled to ask her help. As far as I can discern, it was a result of the Holy Spirit's prompting. I loved this Sister when I lived with her and it seemed necessary that she be a part of this saga. Thank you, Sister, for your great effort toward the success of this book.

I must also mention that when I contacted her, the first comment she made was, "I've elevated you at the altar every day since you left the Convent." Sister, to you and all the others who have prayed for me over the years, I am deeply and humbly grateful! No wonder my life has been so blessed!

One of my classmates was also on that first mission with me. She was our housekeeper and a very good one! The only thing I ever had against her was pickled beets. I hated those things. The farmers must have hated them also because they brought them to her by the buckets. Apparently the only way she knew how to preserve them was by pickling. I haven't eaten one since.

She and I laugh about our way of unwinding after a busy week. I'd come in from school tired and she'd often be trying to vacuum with a vacuum cleaner that had seen better days. Once as she was using an attachment on her hands and knees, we both sat under the dining room table and commiserated with each other. It must have made quite a sight!

When I saw this Sister recently, she said, "Don't tell about the worm!" If I lived to be a hundred, I will never forget and maybe never forgive her for the worm episode! I am a nature nut; (big nut). One time I found a huge Cecropia caterpillar stretched out at least six inches long on the sidewalk. I ran back to get a container. By the time I returned, my lousy classmate had squashed it dead!

Once when the two of us were in the novitiate together, a classmate, upon getting dressed in the morning, found a bat, as in the order of Chiroptera, clinging to her black postulant habit. Being the good nun that she was to become, she did not wish to be late for Chapel. She wrapped the bat up in her habit and put on her Sunday habit. After prayers and breakfast, she went to take her daily habit and captive bat outside. She had the habit out on the patio but there was no bat! We hunted the dorm with a fine tooth comb. No bat.

The day passed and bedtime came, after prayers at night no one spoke. This was a time called the Great Silence. It was a penance offered until after breakfast each morning.

We were all getting ready to doze off that evening when someone said, "Turn on the light. There's a bat in here!"

We looked and looked. No bat. Off went the light and at least some of us were dozing off again when another country was heard from. "Turn on the light. There's a bat in here!" Another search – no bat!

Once more, I was ready to fall off to sleep when I had the strange sensation of something crawling up the side of my bed. I said, "Turn on the light; there's a bat in here," and Sister, of the rolled-up captured morning bat, said, "Oh, go to sleep; there's no bat in here!"

Very loudly, I yelled, "Turn on the <u>damn</u> light!" The light went on as I raised myself up on my hands, Brother bat slithered onto the bed, wings spread to the area of where my midriff had been, over the pillow, and down to the floor. I screamed and cried and shook, making a real hysterical scene. As I ran out of the dorm, I looked back. There were nine nuns in their nightgowns, beating the hell out of one tiny, little bat, and I was crying so hard that I couldn't laugh! I haven't liked bats since.

Once when I was still at home, one of my little nieces found a hibernating bat hanging on the wall of the oat bin in winter. She brought it in and yelled, "Grandma, Grandma, look I found a little baby devil!"

I was totally useless in sacristan work. It was a guaranteed surety that if I did whatever had to be done around the altar, it was wrong. I couldn't seem to ever get things right.

(Rumble) Forgive me, dear brother, Red, but I was so much like you. Remember when Dad told you to harness the horse, Old Jan, and you put the harness on backward and couldn't figure out what was wrong? Remember when you drove a loaded hay wagon down the hill by the gravel pit and tore out the new gate in the fence, while going through?

You were so wonderful in my eyes but you could sometimes do such stupid things. That's the reason I loved you so much. Even when you proved your worth on the international scene, you were still humble. (Now I know your three kids must think I've flipped.) They don't know who I'm talking about – because after all, you're their father! It takes us about fifty years to get a decent perspective on life! In one way or another, all the members of your family have always reached up to you.

My oldest son is so much like you. If I hadn't known you, I might have exterminated this lad as he was growing up. He'd come home with straight A's but could be so exasperating in every-day life. Once while he was in his teens, we were fed up with how he did his homework. The T.V. would be on. He'd be lying on the floor, watching, while his feet were on the couch. He left the room one night and I angrily grabbed his notebook. One look at it and Dad and I humbly went back to reading our newspaper. Neither of us could have reproduced his homework.

# Twenty-Five

## FUN DAYS

*B*ack to that first mission - Holy Angels in Darboy. We used to eat our meal, wash our dishes in a pan that was passed around, and reset the table with plates and cups upside down. Great Convent custom! How I used to wish I dared to do this in my married life!

The first time the Superior was gone, we were all talk, talking excitedly at the table about some new "scoop." Out of the corner of my eye, I saw the white table cloth turning red. Sister's famous beet juice was running all over the tablecloth. I hadn't turned my plate right side up!

One Christmas, we were each given three dollars. We exchanged names for Christmas gifts. My classmate had my name and bought goldfish. The area water contained a great deal of sulphur. Sister desperately tried to keep my goldfish alive. We were at Darboy and the water had a terribly rotten egg odor. It killed her fish. She had to melt 'snow' to get safe water for them. She hid them behind her bed in her bedroom so that I wouldn't see them.

We opened our presents on Christmas Eve so that all her fish didn't belly-up before I got them. One of them lived so long that I finally flushed it down the toilet to avoid taking care of it!

I bought one of the Sisters a back-scratcher. It was wrapped like a big megaphone. She opened it up and stammered, "Oh, oh, chopsticks!" That was my happiest Christmas in the Convent.

Polio was rampant the first year that we were there, and we didn't open school until mid-October.

While I was teaching, I got the chicken pox. I was one sick cookie. I didn't expect to be so sick. I remember almost fainting that morning at Mass. It was a Saturday. I couldn't eat breakfast because of nausea.

Besides being nauseated, the pain and itching from the pustules was terrible.

A doctor confined me to bed for a week.

He said the disease was much more severe for an adult than for children.

One spring, all five of us came down with the Asian flu. We all had it at the same time. It flattened us low for a week.

The Superior put a bottle of brandy on the bathroom shelf. She said it might help us. No one told me how strong brandy was. Never giving it a thought, I drank a half water glass of brandy.

Being sick and unfamiliar with liquor, I was one drunken nun! I must have slept 10 hours of daytime. I remember not being able to lift my little finger.

When we dragged ourselves to the first meal together after our illness, Sister put a pie on the table. Someone had brought it the day that we had become ill. It was covered completely by a fine mold. We weren't really hungry anyway, <u>you know!</u>

Remember Mrs. You Know? We used to hold our sides not to laugh when she came over. One day she brought a bushel of apples. We thanked her dubiously. She said, "Well, you know, Sisters, the pigs, you know, would just have gotten them anyway; you know, if I hadn't brought them to you, you know!"

One time when the superior was gone, I felt the need to celebrate. I was at the top of the stairs. For some reason, I was sitting on the step. I let myself slide down in exuberation. Darn near broke my tailbone! I was never tempted to do that again!

We had a Sister with us who was always neat and proper. She had spent a bigger part of Saturday washing and ironing her habit. She wore it the next day. Someone at the table passed her the bowl of creamed peas. The bowl was cracked and just as it reached her; it split in half, dumping its contents on her lap. Now, tell me that wasn't funny. My wicked sense of humor has to have a lid on it to this day.

I loved teaching at Darboy! At the time it was a rural school. The kids gave me a run for my money, but I loved them. Back to the pain and crap. I was woefully short of money by now. The Community didn't know that; and again, I was too proud to tell them.

One section of our science book was about insects. The students brought in a lot of moth cocoons. We pinned them up on the bulletin board that crossed the front of the room.

Because the classroom was warm all winter the moths hatched out too early in spring.

One time Father Baier was teaching religion and kids all pointed to the board. "Sister, Sister!" There was a huge Cecropia moth dripping down the bulletin board unto Father's shoulder.

One student told me he could find all kinds of cocoons while on his paper route.

He discovered that what he thought were cocoons, were gray milkweed pods.

He cut out a picture of a big moth, wrapped it in gauze, and then tree leaves. He glued these on a twig.

If he hadn't been so excited, I might not have caught on.

"Ster", what kind of a cocoon do you think it is?"

"Tom, I think it's a humbug!" So I suggested he tie it on a bush outside so the kids coming back from their homes after breakfast would find it. It was to be a big joke!

The kids found it alright. They took it to the bathroom and cut it open. Poor Tom was in tears! He had worked so hard to make his practical joke!

I was later told that because I was teaching, all my physical needs should have been paid by the Community.

It was time to take my first vows and become a real nun. I was broke. My shoes had holes in them and no amount of polish would cure the situation. I didn't dare go up to the altar in ugly run-down shoes. So, I did the least humiliating thing that I could think of and that almost killed me! I wrote to my brother and begged him for money for new shoes. Well, actually, I just asked. He was more than willing to help me. But to me it sure felt like <u>begging</u>. I guess I don't like that either!

# Twenty-Six

## HELL ON EARTH

*I* went back for my third year on my first mission. It became the saddest year of my life.

The summer before, I had my first home visit; it was for ten days. I could have gone home alone but I knew that some of my family would like to have torn me apart. I took a Sister companion along for protection.

I would have loved to have been in the cars that drove by our house to note the relatives' reaction to what they saw one day. They didn't stop; I was told, because they were aware of Dad's long-standing anger over this whole "nun" thing. When they went by, I had my habit pinned up in back and I was manning the cultivator while Dad led the horse. I didn't know why he wanted me to handle the cultivator but I later understood that it was too difficult for him.

When I left home, I told Dad goodbye as he was carrying pails of milk. He set them down and hugged and kissed me.

He said, "When will you be home again?"

The last time that I saw my Dad, July, 1957.
He died in March, 1958.

I said, "In five years, Dad."

"That's a long time," he replied. "I might not be here then."

"Oh, Dad," I retorted, "You'll be kicking around another twenty years!"

"No," he said, "I don't think so."

Late one March evening, the phone rang. One of the Sisters' brothers had been critically ill and was expected to die. When Sister called for me, I thought she needed my support. I think that I could have died of shock when she told me my father was dead.

How many times am I allowed to say that I adored my Dad? How many times dare I tell you that the feeling was mutual? It was just that I heard God calling me and I answered; -- that was the wedge that split Dad and me apart.

Sister Superior offered me sympathy and I refused it. I locked up and couldn't cry or scream. I was so mad at God, that if I could have gotten my hands around His neck, I would have choked Him, like I used to want to choke my mother to silence her. Now it was God and God alone that I wanted to shut up forever. I never wanted to hear His voice again.

Our God is a great God and He can handle our puny temper tantrums and anger. God answers in ways that we cannot fathom.

At that moment and for years later, all I felt was that God lied to me! He and I, or apparently just I, had a pact or covenant if you will.

In the Old Testament, God's people broke their convent with God. In my view, at this time, in our New Testament era – God had broken His covenant with me – and I was madder than hell!

I thought God and I had this nailed down. I would be a good nun. God would see to it that on Dad's death bed, I would be there to love and comfort Dad. My father would forgive and comfort me for running off after the Divine "Hound of Heaven."

This is what happened. Dad had a serious bout of "indigestion" all night. My parents went to see the doctor whose office was twenty-two miles away.

In those days, if you weren't dead already, walking up the steep steps to any doctor's office would clinch the deal.

Mom went to pick up some needed items at my youthful haunt, where the Brides of Christ just might happen to be, Woolworth's.

The doctor took Dad's blood pressure and told him he'd be dead before night if he didn't go right to the hospital.

My Dad answered by saying, "If I'm going to die, I'm not going to raise a hospital bill doing it!"

He went downstairs, shoveled snow to get the car to move, and drove home. He never told Mom what the doctor said or she would have forced him to go to the hospital.

The doctor later told my Mother that he was sorry, but he just didn't know how to handle such a strong-willed man.

When Dad got home, he started to change clothes. Then he said, "Well, the doctor said that I should take it easy, so maybe I'll go lay down awhile."

An hour later, Mom was scrubbing the kitchen floor. She heard noise in the bedroom and called in, "What are you doing in there, dying?"

She went in to check and Dad had had a massive cerebral

hemorrhage. He died instantly. The date was March 9, 1958.

Part of my shock was due to the fact that he had died at 1:00 p.m., and the phone call about his death came at 9:00 p.m. All of Mom's fears had caused her to build her own walls. First, she was afraid to tell me because she knew how I'd feel. All of her old Protestant fears reared up. Somehow she was afraid the Convent wouldn't let me come home! Even though we now had electricity and a phone at home, I wasn't notified until eight hours later. By that time, I couldn't catch a bus home for another twenty-four hours. When I think about it, I must really have been in shock. I didn't think of calling home and nobody thought of suggesting it. Actually, I guess I wasn't talking to grown-ups – certainly not God's nuns.

I did teach class that next day, though. I remember unlocking my classroom door, in the hallways, while whistling. A fifth grade boy said to me, in the hall, "Gee, Sister, how come you're always so happy?" I remember sitting at the supper table and passing the dishes right on to the next person, because swallowing was out of the question. Poor fellow-nuns, I'm sure they were suffering as much as I was.

Months passed before I began to outwardly grieve. In sheer exasperation, a Superior said to me, "You don't even grieve normally!" I hated her for a long time for that. They say it's the truth that hurts!

Forty years have passed. It was interesting for me to watch, as an outsider would, what has happened to me in my life today.

I've been writing non-stop for four days, with catching only an hour or two of sleep, periodically.

Since writing, "Dad died instantly," I haven't written for ten hours. I've shopped, cooked, eaten and read the newspapers that I missed during the last week and listened to news broadcasts. There was even a fleeting thought that maybe my book had just ended!

It's 2:00 a.m. and my pen moves again.

There are a few comments that I must make about the funeral. My long-time priest friend was between a rock and a hard place.

Father was a holy Church man and my father certainly did not qualify for a church burial in those days. On the other hand, the widow was a very good Christian woman. His daughter was a nun. I'm sure thoughts like this ran through Father's head. "If I don't bury this man in the Church, that nun will surely leave the Church altogether." If he didn't have those thoughts, he should have, because I was silently, defiantly, screaming them at him.

He finally said that he would make the decision on his own, because he was afraid that if he asked the Bishop's permission, it wouldn't be granted. Score one for my good old priest friend!

Including the two Sister Superiors who braved a terrible snow storm to travel over a hundred miles to attend the funeral, there were eight Catholics in the church at Dad's funeral. These people were Mom and I, my brother and his wife, and the priest and his sister, who was his housekeeper and the two nuns.

After my father's funeral, I became really bold and called the Convent. I simply informed the Mother Superior, (didn't ask permission), that I was staying home another week. We were only allowed three days for a parents' funeral.

After all the family left, while I was home alone with Mom, I told her that I wasn't going to go back to the Convent. I was going to learn to drive that car in the garage and I was going to run that damn farm myself.

Mom said, "If you leave the Convent, it's up to you, but for God's sake, don't do it now!

My family couldn't understand my decisions in the past, and if I left the Convent when Dad died, I'd blow their minds twice! So the nun obeyed her mother and obediently returned to the Convent! I've never told anyone that before!

PATRICIA ANN DUDKIEWICZ

Mom and I in a privately owned ravine in Mishicot, 1961.

## Twenty-Seven

## LIKE FOAM – FUN RISES TO THE TOP

It's 3:00 a.m. My husband was just grumbling and making noises in his sleep. I went in, wakened him, and said, "Hon, are you having nightmares?"

"Yah," he said. "There were a bunch of ghosts – you know – ghosts?"

Ain't that amazing now! Some of them must have escaped off these pages!

I was sent to another mission. This was in Mishicot, at Holy Cross School. Once more, the children and I had a love affair.

My biggest problem in the next three years were those "Brides of Christ." I loved them, and there were only four of us on that mission. Each of my other three companions had taught school longer than I had lived. Talk about having an inferiority complex!

I was adamantly sure that no one in <u>their</u> classrooms ever spoke out of turn. None of <u>their</u> students threw spitballs or shot rubber bands around the room. Surely <u>their</u> students all finished their homework.

One sixth grader just batted zero in a math assignment. One afternoon, he had to stay after class and correct his assignment. He was in the library working on it when his mother came for him. I heard her exclaim, "Tommy, an F! Daddy and I spent an hour on that last night!"

There was a ravine near that mission in Mishicot leading into a woods that was full of beech trees. They had real paper thin leaves that resembled elm leaves. In fall, they turned into a deeply burnished leather color. They were gorgeous!

In that ravine blossomed every Wisconsin wild flower that I had ever seen. Some I have not seen since.

I have two snapshots that were taken of my mother and me, separately holding huge bouquets of Dutchman Breeches. The joy of nature just emanates from those pictures. Part of me has always envisioned those as bridal pictures. Both my mother and I have always been wedded to the God whom we first met in the beauty of nature.

There was an active Audubon Club that many of my boys were involved in. They reminded me of aliens from outer space, sometimes when they showed up for school. They wore tall protective boots and gloves. Their pants and jackets were dew-soaked. They helped government workers capture migrating birds in special fine nets in order to conduct bird counts and band certain species.

There were very few migratory bird laws at the time. When we came to the bird chapter in our Science Book, the students taught me. At one time we had a collection of fifty seven properly identified bird nests. The government workers helped the students identify them. It was fall and the birds were done nesting. The workers at the time considered this project helpful to the birds. If there were parasites or diseases in the nest, the birds would pick it up the next season, by re-using the nest.

We fumigated each nest and displayed them in matching white boxes sealed with cellophane. Each nest was labeled and had a corresponding colored drawing of the bird in its natural setting. The girls in the class were responsible for the labeling and drawings. A father of one of the boys constructed display shelves.

These nests belonged to summer bird residents. Our largest nest was a hawk nest and the smallest belonged to the ruby-throated humming bird.

I elaborated the details above for one reason. Only fellow Sisters could appreciate how terribly funny and realistically true the next story is.

The nun who had written our Science text was a wonderful, brilliant, exasperating school supervisor. She came to visit during this glorious educational experience that we were having. We happened to be on the chapter on birds, as one might have incidentally noticed. Besides the nests, about 40 booklets, made by the students about birds they knew, were displayed on the bulletin boards. She spent her visitation hour in my classroom going on and on about geology and rocks!

That kind of happening might have made me ferociously angry at the time, but as years passed, it became hilarious.

Today it's a federal offense to possess a feather, egg, or nest. If prosecuted, there's a five-hundred dollar fine.

(Ramble) When the above law was passed, my six and nine year old sons and I were involved in constructing our own collection. We were doing a mighty fine job of it. The boys were so mad! They said that they were going to dig a big hole in the ground, and cover our collection with plastic so that it wouldn't decay. They weren't going to let any old government tell them what to do with their nests!

My sons never forgave me for giving all those nests to the brothers who climbed those trees and risked their necks for most of that collection, twenty years before. I didn't give my hummingbird nest away for years. I certainly had no premonition that there were to be two special sons in my future or I would have kept that nest. I have never been able to locate one since.

My own relatives have had dozens of hummingbirds nesting in their yards. There's been a big drive to get a nest for me. I've tried climbing those trees myself, studying them through binoculars, leaning out of second-story windows until people thought for sure

I'd kill myself, all to no avail. I've never seen another nest. The nest is the size of half a walnut shell. The inside is lined with dandelion or dryer fuzz. The outside is always layered with grey or green lichen from tree trunks. These are glued on with sticky spider webs.

The people who had found that nest had watched the bird the previous spring as it made its way back and forth from their dryer to their apple tree.

One day that same year, my mother came to visit. I entered my classroom and there were knots of kids around "Tom," the special bird kid! The air was full of tension and excitement.

I said, "What's up, boys?"

"Oh, nothing, 'Ster'."

Mom came in and was seated quietly in the front corner where she could see everything. (God help us!)

Now I wanted to impress her with a good performance.

Also, a diocesan supervisor was in the building. I had double reason to want everything to go well that day.

We said morning prayers. I went to open a drawer in my desk and out flew a sparrow. Up, up, and away! All the girls screamed and all the boys jumped up to catch the bird.

They left it outside and class resumed as normal. Twenty minutes later, I opened the drawer for something else and out flew another bird. Repeat performance!

Just before recess, I opened a side drawer for a book and outburst the third sparrow.

I started recess early to get the screaming masses out into the fresh air in order to release their boundless energy upon the universe.

Tom had to stay in.

I said, "Tom, I think you owe an apology to the classroom and me, when the students come back in." I explained why it was so vital to me that that particular day would have gone well.

The class came back in. Tom went up to the front like a real man. His face was as white as a sheet and he was shaking. I was afraid he might faint. This was his apology, word for word.

"I'm sorry that I brought the birds to school. It was really a bad day. Sister's mother is here and the supervisor is in the building. But the next time that I do something like this, don't all you girls scream!"

I loved my teaching experience at Mishicot. Being the youngest person by about 30-50 years was a very hard situation to cope with.

Religious life at the time was such that you could never leave the grounds alone. On weekends, you had to ask permission to go to the school. To me, it was extremely stifling and restrictive, especially because there was no young sister there to communicate with.

# Twenty-Eight

## ONCE MORE – I LIVE!

This is a wonderful story about two wonderful deceased nuns.

One ran the most congested, confusing, creative classroom on earth. Her name was Sr. Theophane. Every child tutored another child at one time or another. No child left this nun's first and second grade classroom without being able to pick up an unknown song for the rest of her or his life, with the ability to sing it on sight. They all knew their do-re-mi's. I have still never learned to do that. Too bad I wasn't <u>her</u> student.

This Sister also made the most perfect gladiola bouquets for the church that were ever made. She tried and tried to show me how to do it and I failed and failed. She'd line up those glads in their baskets and then she'd say, "Now, you have to fill in the middle."

On her feast day, I got revenge. I made a gladiola bouquet for our dining room table. In the middle, I stuck a toilet brush. "So there, Sister! I filled in the middle!"

The third and fourth grade teacher at school was Sr. Theodora. She was quiet and unassuming. She was shorter than many of her students. Actually, much of the world could have totally missed her existence. She methodically taught phonics and drilled Math cards. Here's a shocking revelation to the younger generation of today. Back then, it was not uncommon for a nun to have over fifty students in two grades in the same classroom.

I taught the fifth and sixth grade students.

No student came out of those two nuns' classrooms who couldn't read books or master math at their own level.

I had at least two students with I.Q. scores in the low seventies. That's classified as barely teachable. Those two students could read orally like no other students that I remember, regardless of how high their I.Q.'s might have been. Now, they perhaps didn't comprehend what they read but, by golly, read they could! They couldn't figure out Math story problems but they certainly did well on Math computation.

Remember the book, <u>Why Johnny Can't Read</u>? Well, Johnny never had those two teachers!

Dear public school teachers of the nineties – nuns back then had two recess duties outside, daily; autumn, winter and spring. We either had lunchroom duty or noon playground, which allowed us twenty-five minutes tops for our own personal care and luncheon. Frequently, luncheon got the short shift.

We prayed that the weather would be nice enough so that we didn't have to spend the noon hour in close quarters with those little angels. If we did, it meant that we were stuck inside with their noise and overload of carbon dioxide. It was a treat to open the doors and windows and get a fresh change of air while the room was empty.

We also had the roles of Phy. Ed. teacher, nurse, and art and music instructors.

If the parents brought their children early in the morning or didn't pick them up after classes, we became their baby sitters.

In those days, we started this whole ball a'rolling by attending daily Mass with this bunch of squirming humanity. I'm sure some older nun out there is shaking her head and saying, "Did you know that some of us did all that, in addition to being principal of the school and superior of the mission?" Good Lord!

And <u>you kids</u> thought that <u>you</u> had it rough because you <u>went</u> to a

Catholic School? Look at the flip side of the picture.

There are so many jokes and tales about discipline in those schools. Some nuns and some Orders definitely went overboard. For those, we are all sorry and ashamed. For my own mistakes, I have deep regret. On the whole, however, those women poured their hearts out for their students, considering the odds that they were up against.

One of my friends who left the Convent had a Master's degree. She later taught in a large public school. She could hardly adjust to the change. She had less than half the students that she had ever taught. There was no playground duty. There were class preparation periods, plus regular art, music and gym instructors. In addition, this teacher was paid an unbelievable salary.

This bit of information might startle you. At least in our Order, the nuns never had money. We had no money. We sent in a request slip once a year for what we considered necessities. And one did not always get what one asked for, or perhaps not the total list we had requested. If gifts or money were given to us, they were turned into Community property.

Granted we had free room and board. That was just a given. However, that in itself was governed by the Spirit of Poverty. Many gifts were shuttled off to poor people.

When I was teaching, the parishes paid a fifty dollar a month fee for each teaching nun. That money went toward the living expenses on the Mission; any leftover went to support the old and sick Sisters at the Convent Motherhouse.

So-o- my fellow lay Catholics – when the collection is taken annually to help the old, retired and in many ways, disappearing religious nuns, think deeply. Dig even more deeply into your wallet. Nuns today are primarily old nuns. There are not many younger nuns left to support their needs. Those old nuns are not on Social Security, for the most part. They're on Divine Providence and your gratitude!

# Twenty-Nine

## LOOKING BACK

*I* was stationed at the next mission, St. Boniface in De Pere, for two years. Teaching and kids were fine! The story that overwhelms this period of time involves cooking.

Dear Sister Lawrence was a friend of mine from years back. She did not have many friends. She lacked social skills and she scared the hell out of most of the nuns. Sister came up the hard way. All of her life before entering the Convent had been a living hell. I knew this.

There were probably only two things in life that Sister Lawrence understood. One was prayer and the other was work. She was beyond doubt a master, in both of those subjects.

Now in Lawrence's eye, education and teaching did not in any way qualify as work, much less hard work. She worked like a horse and any nun who knew her would agree with me.

It's strange when I think about it. The only photographer's photograph that I have of any nun is of Sister Lawrence. I'm willing to bet that it was the only professional picture ever taken of her. The Convent had celebrated a big anniversary and they must have roped and tied her to get a picture. Anyway, it's a great picture. I stole it off the bulletin board at her funeral.

Sister Lawrence and I liked each other. She always called me by my family name. Her half-sister was married to my uncle. She probably considered me a relative. To her I was McKinney.

After I left the convent the first time, Sister used to write to me long, newsy letters. I once had a ten-page letter from her filled on both sides. The general flow of the letter went like this: picked however many hundred pounds of potatoes, (she helped run the Convent garden at the time), canned nine hundred quarts of raspberries, froze so much asparagus, canned six hundred quarts of corn, etc., etc.

At the time, Sister Lawrence's own mother relied on my letters for news from Sister.

(Ramble) When I first went to the convent out of eighth grade, Sisters Hermana and Lawrence were both cooks at the Motherhouse. I was drowning in an environment totally foreign to me. Sr. Hermana fed me those notoriously delicious molasses cookies that she was famous for making. Sister Lawrence let me help her in the bakery making prune-filled ponchies and poppy seed kolachies. Sister Anna – dear old Sister Anna. She was old. She had been very stern in her prime, but she had greatly mellowed by the time that I met her. She and I planted flowers and weeded garden beds for days at a time. Once, one of my classmates received a package of special flower seeds from her father. She dug a ten-inch hole and put all the seeds in it. Sister Anna and I chuckled over that often.

Sister Carmella was in charge of the large Convent garden. I often worked alone with her, and in big groups of other Sisters, taking care that the vegetables overcame the weeds. I was particularly in awe of the large root cellar used for fresh preservation. I had never seen one before, so Sister Carmella was delighted with my enthusiasm.

Together those nuns plotted to keep me away from Sister Barbara's laundry. An hour or two was all that nun could abide of me!

God, I loved those women and still do today! Well, -- at times I disliked some of them, but absence makes the heart grow fonder. Isn't it true? Almost all of them are dead. Time and changing hormones mellow us all – even me, Thank God!

Our Order's religious habit was changing like many after Vatican II. Soon they would be dressed in lay clothing and have the option to take back their former names.

Taken in 1964.
Sister Maureen.

## Thirty

## AND A COOKING WE WILL GO!

Sister Lawrence was the housekeeper at St. Boniface in De Pere, this new mission that I was on. At that time, I didn't know how to crack an egg or peel a potato efficiently. Sister Lawrence had to have back surgery and they carted her off to the hospital and the powers that be. Now if I had the situation sized up right, no one was sorry to see her go! How they thought we'd survive without her, was a mystery to me at the time. I loved her much but in general, she was a real royal pain.

It was Christmas vacation. Now I wasn't on Cortisone then, but I had this wild inspiration! There were thirteen nuns on the mission. I heard myself volunteering to make Christmas dinner. I'm sure the Sisters were relieved to have some fool volunteer.

A friend, who knew less about cooking, if possible, than I did, volunteered to help me.

Another nun in this house had raised her siblings when her parents died. She was reputedly an excellent cook. I didn't know this, or I might have failed on the spot.

We prepared roast stuffed turkey, potatoes, gravy, yams; you name it. The glorious encore was something that I've never made since. Baked Alaska! Are you familiar with the beautiful picture of that dessert in the Betty Crocker Cookbook? It looked just like that! You made a sponge cake, piled various colors and flavors of ice cream in a bowl, formed it in a half sphere and placed it on top of the cake. Then you froze the whole thing. Just before serving, you would frost curls of egg meringue all over the ice cream. This was then put into the oven and baked to a golden brown delight.

Everything was perfect until it came time to carve the bird. I used a bread knife and couldn't understand why I had so much "sawdust." As I was carving, the Sister with experience came in, and straightened me out.

At the end of the year this Sister and I were reminiscing. She was absolutely astonished to learn that when I started I had known "zilch" about cooking. That explained the "sawdust" to her and the time that I served roast beef, for sandwiches, sliced a half an inch thick!

One very important tidbit... In all the years that I cooked in the convent, I don't ever recall making a grocery list. I planned menus around what was in the pantry and freezer, from the annual parish food shower. That was good life training. If you don't have a certain item, improvise or do without!

(Ramble) I raised my sons to know that there's nothing they cannot cook. Any normal human being can pick up a cookbook and follow a recipe. One of my sons is a phenomenal home chef. The other son and his fiancé are just embarking together on their journey to experience the joy of cooking.

The day after Christmas, dinner time was approaching. There was no sign of any movement in the kitchen. I, for one, was hungry and the situation was getting desperate, at least in my eyes. So, once again, I asked, "Sister, would you like me to make a meal?"

Her answer was, "I assumed that you would do it, until I told you not to!"

Oh-h-h, now that was a different story! Any fool can make one good meal. No one ever said, "Stop," so I cooked for twelve to fifteen people for the next five years.

Someone made a bad mistake. When others asked how we were doing without a housekeeper, they said, "We don't even miss Sister Lawrence".

Now that was absolutely untrue, but it was one of those stupid sayings that slip out of people's mouths unintentionally. It got back to Sister Lawrence and my name was anathema.

Now, remember when I said that I'm a coward by nature?

Well, I went to the hospital to face the "Beast." She took one look at me and deliberately turned her back! So I pulled myself up by my bootstraps and went around the bed to face her.

"See here, Sister Lawrence. I know what you're mad about. Some idiot, who doesn't have the slightest inkling as to what she was talking about, apparently ran off at the mouth. There's no way that I could begin to take your place and I'm just cooking! You did everything." Well, we were friends for life, after that.

Actually, I went to bed with a Betty Crocker Cookbook for years. Besides not knowing anything about cooking, I was now responsible for the nutritional needs of over a dozen people. This was no longer a joke!

## Thirty-One

## TALES OUT OF SCHOOL

God played his games, but later when cooking was essential to married life, I was a pro. Then, God rewarded me! He gave me a husband who washed clothes and cleaned house!

My husband not only washes, weather permitting, he hangs them outside. He even folds and puts them away. To top that off, he's fast!

I am the envy of any woman who knows how lucky I am. I haven't washed a floor in 45 years. Actually, I have seldom dusted or vacuumed. That's probably partly because I've proven myself unqualified, and partly because although my husband wouldn't admit it, I think he likes to do it.

He lived his life in this house. When he came home from the Navy, his mother was sick. Most of his life he's taken care of this house.

Now, if my kids could get me to pick up my pile of Kleenex and reading material that always dominates the floor by my chair, we'd have a happier household!

How about some cooking stories? These are <u>early</u> experiences. In time, I matured; I'm still in the process!

We had an institutional gas stove. The pilot light kept blowing out on account of an open kitchen window. Some of the nuns felt duty-bound to keep that pilot light lit. They'd light it as they passed through the kitchen during the day. Then they'd lay the match stick on the spoon holder.

The parish priests did not have a housekeeper at the time so they frequently joined us for dinner. One day, as the old pastor helped himself to the first-serving of a casserole, my helper and I wanted to die of embarrassment. As he put a heaping spoonful onto his plate, we could see a large matchstick clinging to the bottom of the spoon. The dish was handed to my helper and she surreptitiously retrieved the culprit. Neither of us giggled or ever mentioned it to the others!

An almost full gallon of dried apricots was given to us by the school lunch program. According to regulations, if something was opened, it was to be discarded. Well, it really was discarded, next door! Having the vow of Poverty we saw waste as a sin.

I cooked up the apricots, sugared them, and dished out fourteen sauce dishes of fruit.

As my Sister companion walked in, just to be nice to her, I said, "Taste the apricots and see what you think!"

Now I knew that they were perfect. My pride and palate had established that before I "humbly" asked her opinion!

Well, she said that they were too tart. So, she emptied them back in a big bowl and added a cup of SALT! She was one surprised cookie when she discovered that her taste buds weren't testing sugar!

First, I was mad. Now I had no sauce. Seconds later, we were both doubled over howling in laughter.

At another mission, my all-time most long-standing friend was my helper. We had mutually hated each other when we first met. She and two of her classmates were stuck cleaning the huge Motherhouse, alone. My ten classmates and I were stationed at a new formation house doing nothing, as she saw it. The first time I met her she was freely expressing her mind to a fellow classmate. To my ears, she sounded very uncharitable and I decided that I didn't like her. It was a two-way street for a number of years.

We finally got acquainted on my third mission. We were quite a cooking pair. Someone thought that Sister and I were just too friendly with each another. On the other hand, this person couldn't understand how we could be Christian and be so mean to each other! I got called on the carpet that summer. I was taken completely aback; Webster says, "aback" means to have the sails blown back against the mast!" Well, I really mean aback! I was grumbling out loud to some Sister, nursing my wounds. The windows in all the rooms were open. I had just said, "Can you believe that? I've never even had an uncharitable thought about Sister!"

I must have been quite vocal because from another open window, I heard Sister Agnes' voice, "Too bad I can't say the same thing about you!"

One Thanksgiving, I took the left-over turkey off the bone and boiled the carcass for soup. It smelled delicious. Not being able to leave well enough alone, I added new water and boiled it the second time. Only this time, I forgot about it until a Sister came running up the stairs, "Sister, Sister, are you burning something?" It smelled like a crematorium!

I paralyzed at the sight of a whole chicken in the freezer. I didn't want anyone to know how stupid I was. I wrote and asked my Mom, who lived a hundred and fifty miles away, to come by bus and show me how to proceed with cutting up the bird. She did.

While Mom was visiting, she made corn muffins and chili for our crowd. She said to me, "The acidity of the tomato in the chili can be cut by adding a little sugar." So she took care of it. "The muffins will taste better with a little sugar added, she said.

I took one bite of each at the table. The other nuns all seemed to be eating, oblivious to any problem.

I looked at Mom, "She sure is aging," I thought. She looked so bleak and far away.

All of a sudden, she burst out with, "That was <u>salt</u> in that canister on the cupboard, wasn't it?"

The next week, she sent me a little package with instructions for me to label our canisters!

One of my housekeeping friends was not a good speller. I always admired the fact that every time she wrote a letter, she had a dictionary in hand. This amazed me, because at the time I remember thinking, "If you don't know how to spell a word, how can you look it up in the dictionary?"

One day she called me and said, "I'm looking at this recipe here. It sounds like a lot of lye for soup."

I said, "Sister, what is it called?" I couldn't imagine any recipe for soup that would call for lye.

She answered, "Well, you know, s-o-a-p!"

When I first started cooking, someone gave us a large bucket of perch fillets.

I read Betty Crocker and tackled the job. It seemed to be going ok. It was a large commercial cooking stove. I had four pans of fish frying. In the middle, I had two huge platters lined with paper toweling.

I was almost done frying and heaping the platters when flames hit my paper toweling. Out I ran with two flaming platters trying to enflame my large plastic collar.

My companion helper was laughing when I returned, having somehow rescued the fish. I heard someone say "Laugh you damn fool!" Now, that wasn't a nice nun inside of me who spoke those words!

## Thirty-Two

### ALL OF LIFE IS A GIFT!

(Ramble) At the time I'm writing this, I've lived 80 years. I have severe arthritis. Plain and simple, I think I look and feel old, physically. Some fellow workers still register sincere surprise when they discover my age.

People of all ages relate to my youthful spirit, and along with me, ignore my physical handicaps. On the other hand, older fellow employees and elderly customers are encouraged or inspired, if you will, by my dogged determination. They know that we share the same common aging processes and are encouraged by the humor with which they are met.

I've hated my canes since the day they became necessary evils! I am forever leaving them behind. I may have walked somewhere pushing a grocery cart for support. Perhaps, I'd just had a pain pill and was able to walk some distance, forgetting my canes.

All of a sudden, there I am, and those stupid canes are way over there, and I can't get back to them! That's why I insist that the very fact of our existence, if not goaded against, and if we're willing to allow it, teaches all of us humility.

I don't <u>like</u> to ask a young person to tie my shoe. I don't <u>like</u> to have a friend bring me coffee or worse yet! – wipe up the coffee that

I just tried to burn them with. But we are bound together in this Mystical Body of Christ. How can a Christian give, if fellow-Christians refuse to receive? Humility is one of the oils that keep the Mystical Body of Christ lubricated, as I see it.

I've been so embarrassed by this cane bit. At work, I try to hide the need by pushing an empty grocery cart whenever possible. I get such excruciating pain in my joints at the most unexpected times that without canes, I could faint or collapse and break some other vital part of my anatomy!

One day a nine-year old girl said, "How come you use canes?"

I replied, "Oh, honey, I've used them for a long time. I just try to hide them from people!"

She looked at me with the adorable innocence that only a child can have, and said, "Why would you ever try to hide something if it helps you to walk?"

I finally said to myself, "Why would I?" Since then, I have had peace on that front. Thank you, sweet little girl, for your ageless wisdom!

Having been raised alone with older parents, I learned authority and stability. I spent over a decade absorbing the vitality of youth in my classrooms. I learned to go out into the world of mice and men. There I captured, or better yet, was captured by the man in my life who is by no means a mouse!

Then came twenty-seven years (with my obviously beloved sons), from the agony of birth, to the joy and anticipation of their future marriages which are approaching with rapidity.

This has produced an electric personality which leaps through life while my body drags around on pills and surgeries and canes.

Perhaps because I had a grown-up childhood, I prize childhood enough to create it in my own adulthood. I've always enjoyed the mentality and company of youth. Because I was thirty-seven and forty respectively when I had my own children, I have never lost touch with childhood and adolescence.

I grew up with older parents and I relate well to the elderly. So for some of my fellow workers, who tease me about adopting everyone -- for those who say, "I go into the store and if I want to find you, I just look for the table with a crowd around it;" this is my explanation. I've offered it to you with humility.

Before I left the Convent, I loved children. I was afraid of adults, I taught children and in those days had very little to do with grown-ups. At one time, I really didn't like people, certainly not the adult kind.

Now, those people take over. There's a running joke about all my boyfriends! They start at age two and proceed into the nineties. Their women shop and they visit and taste samples. I'm a good cook and married to a man whom I love. So these men can eat my samples and safely flirt!

I have never met any man that I would, even in my wildest fantasy, dream of being married to, other than my husband. In one way or another, they all pale in comparison.

Several times, as my boys were growing up and thinking that they were better than their father, I told them that if they grew up to be half the man that their father was, I would be proud of them. I meant it. I once mentioned this at work. A very distinguished looking gentleman said to me, "Do you know what high praise that is of your husband?" My answer was, "Yes, sir – I do!"

Every once in a while I get a glimpse of something in those boys of mine that tells me that they have already passed the half-way mark!

When it comes to the men in my life, I have no humility – only pride.

I've learned through experience, that absolutely nothing is ours. I think that I am honestly aware that my husband and sons are just loaned to me. I don't deserve them, or have the right to try to control them. They belong to God, and I'm patient enough to know that when things in their lives go differently than I might wish, that they too are involved in a checkers game with God.

I've not only watched God play that game – I've been deeply engrossed in its intrigue. I know who will win the game the men in my life are engaged in, even if they maybe don't realize that they are involved with the Master.

I once had a beautiful high soprano voice that I thought was mine. I've lost it! Several times in my life, I have totally lost my joy and sense of humor. Now, wouldn't you think that you owned that? Just recently, and several other times in my life, I lost my ability to breathe on my own. What I'm trying to say to all who read this is, "All is Gift, All!" And for all of that, we must say, write or sing, "Our Magnificat," – "My soul is glorified by the Lord!"

I --, we, -- have gifts; -- we're accountable for their use. The writing of this book is a gift to me. I hope that it proves to be a gift to those who read it.

# Thirty-Three

## WARM UP IN THE OCEANS OF MY SOUL

Remember how I said that I felt strung out, pulled taut, ready to snap, as a result of the prescribed eighty milligrams of Cortisone a day? It was literally given to me to help me inhale the very breath of life. By now, you know the struggle for breath and life is not new to me in a number of ways.

I just needed an alternate word, so I looked up "extension" in the dictionary. It says among other things, "The act of stretching or pulling taut," etc. etc.!

I had been pulled so-o-o taut that when my medication was gradually reduced, there was all this relaxed, stretched out energy that is now flowing out in the form of organized ink!

Having been a farmer's daughter, I'm familiar with fence-making (both agricultural and psychological!). I know that the physical act of tightly stretching, pulling, or bending wire causes heat. Heat causes meltdown. How's that for melting a glacier?

I'm sort of having my own little "El Nino." Not the same, but for me, there is a definite resemblance. There certainly was a warm-up in the oceans of my soul that has resulted in tidal waves and storms within me during this past month that could never have been predicted, not even by me.

My husband is an old "Almanac" amateur weather man. His intimate knowledge of me in the last thirty years left him completely unprepared for the changes in the weather patterns of my soul, when the warm-up came. Like a true-blue old-timer, he stayed put and endured the onslaughts, rather than evacuate!

My thoughts and feelings have released like bolts of lightning. They strike in the darkness of non-sleep. They pour out in the light of day. I've walked around, working or relaxing with notebook in hand, capturing those thoughts in ink as they came pouring out of the galaxy of my being.

As I sit looking at those chapters clipped together on my huge dining room table, I wonder how I can join them so that they make sense to anyone who might for one reason or another, find themselves reading this book.

The very thought of this book was conceived, due to medication. I have <u>lived</u> the book but it would have stayed frozen within, without the Warm-Up. My medication has been cut down. I am now taking ten milligrams of Cortisone a day. By the end of this month, my system will have been weaned from the drug.

The doctor explained to me that I needed Cortisone to live. I really had been very ill. The Cortisone was needed to open the airways. Normally, the adrenal glands produce adrenalin that keeps the heart beating and the airways open. Under the circumstances, the normal activity of the system was not sufficient. Cortisone takes over the adrenal system. If one quit taking the Cortisone suddenly, death could occur because the adrenal system has shut down. So it takes time and a gradation of the dosage to safely reduce the cortisone and allow the body to return to its normal procedure.

The rehabilitative nurse who came to check on me from the insurance company was wonderful. They had known upon calling and tape recording our conversation, early in the occurrence, that I was very ill, because I was gasping for breath and could hardly speak. She said, "It's just one of those things that can happen unexpectedly. It surely was a <u>freak</u> accident." I agree.

I just checked my friend Webster for the meaning of freak. This is what is written among other things, "a sudden and apparently causeless change or turn of the mind." Perhaps, "melt down??"

This book has sat on the back of my work table for 17 years. It has had time to age and mellow. Now it's time to be published!

# Thirty-Four

## REMINISCING

In the past two weeks, whenever my subconsciously released torrents of thoughts surfaced to my conscious, I have let my pen catch those thoughts. My table is covered with clipped pages that I just have to connect in coherent form. In flipping through all of them, I discovered that, lo and behold, I'm on my own to make sense out of the worst years of my life. Hey, subconscious! How about a little light on the subject?

They were the best of years and the worst of years. I loved my students with a passion. They contributed to both my downfall and my salvation. The first year, on my last mission, as I perhaps mentioned before, I had forty-eight eighth grade students. I loved those kids, fought with them, and agonized over them in prayer. Many, many of them confided those terrifyingly ghastly secrets that haunt all teenagers. They shared their loves and hatreds and deep dark sins with me. This left me feeling torn apart because it complicated things in the classroom for me. These students' lives intertwined with one another in many cases. This microcosm of our classroom prepared them and me, for the great macrocosm that faced us all, when we left those protective walls for the future that loomed unsuspectingly ahead of each of us.

By far the most momentous experience of these three years was one of the most frightening in all of American history.

The breaking news, as the noon recess came to a close, was: "The President of the United States has been shot by an assassin." This announcement was soon to be followed by the tearful trembling broadcaster's voice, forever to be etched in stone in our hearts and memories. "My fellow Americans, the President of the United States, John F. Kennedy, is dead!"

I doubled over in cold shock and nausea. My mind couldn't comprehend such reality. The girls in my classroom went hysterical. They boys were torn between shock at Kennedy's death and what seemed to them, the absurd reaction of the girls.

This was during the era of the "Beatles." The same girls swooned and sobbed and fainted over their musical idols. This was just too much for the male mind to absorb. Some of the boys laughed, which sent the girls in droves, to cry in the bathrooms and halls.

I went to calm the girls down and explain that the boys weren't being blasphemous – they just didn't know how to deal with their emotions.

Several years ago, a woman approached me at work. I didn't recognize her at first. She said to me, "Do you remember where you were when Kennedy was shot?" It was probably around the 30th anniversary of his death. I know that I heard T.V. announcers asking the same question at that time.

Thinking that the lady was just a stranger posing a rhetorical question, I said, "Oh, yes, no one could ever forget where they were when they heard that announcement."

She answered, "Well, I was where you were that day. Remember how we girls were all mad at the boys and we were in the bathroom crying and screaming?"

I said, "Oh, the boys felt the same way you did but they just didn't know how to handle their emotions."

And this woman, now in her early forties, exclaimed, "That's exactly what you said thirty years ago!!"

Isn't that beautiful?

There was a lot of internal pain and anguish within me during those last years that defy description. I buried my pain in classroom art. We produced bulletin boards of breath-taking beauty. Many of the students were gifted with writing, music and artistic abilities. Their creative growth promoted healing within me.

One thing that I greatly missed in these years was directing the choir. We had so many accomplished musicians on the staff that I wasn't needed in that area. No one could have imagined what a gap that left in my search for wholeness.

Music, and my own voice coming from deep within my gut, was a balm to all the joys and pains of my existence.

To be able to draw that same balm from deep within the guts of students, was a wonder never ceasing to me. But God had other moves in mind.

On my previous mission, I had directed for a nun who was top organist, bar none, in my mind. I had no musical training but she had chosen me for her choir director.

There was a mirror above the organ. I stood behind her facing the large choir that flanked her on both sides. Many of the hymns we sang were in three-part harmony. These were also the days of Latin hymns and Gregorian chant.

Basically I'm a follower, not a leader. I'll go to no end, out of my way, to side-step a leadership role. Well, this nun would not play a note unless I directed. She was exasperating! If I absent-mindedly forgot to move my hand, there was silence. I couldn't fathom an organist who followed a director! My concept of music, up till then, was that the choir or singers were to keep up to the organist. I have never before, nor since, heard a choir that compared with what our combination produced.

(Ramble) When I was a child, we had an old Brunswick Victrola. It was supposed to be spring-wound. Well, my older siblings killed that.

Now rumor has it that my voice sounded like a cackling crow

when I was little. There were albums and more albums of all those wonderful classic 78 RPM records. There were compositions by Beethoven, Mozart, Shubert, and Straus, etc. There were great singers like Schumann Heink, John McCormick and Ethel Barrymore.

I vividly remember when the Black woman, Marian Anderson, was refused permission to sing at some national Woman's Society, and Eleanor Roosevelt invited her to sing at the White House. I also remember when Kate Smith took the public by storm with her rendition of "God Bless America."

Well, anyway, that old Victrola was broken. So to play those records, I had to stand and run the disk around and around with my index finger. It was wonderful music! Remember, we didn't have electricity and we couldn't afford batteries for radio. Necessity is the Mother of invention! In the process, I learned to sing on pitch!

Some nuns, in the choirs in which we sang, didn't understand why I always had to be near enough to the organ to have my hand on it. I had learned as a child to sing by reading the vibrations with my hand on the record. My other arm and hand were leaning on the Victrola. My body absorbed the music and transferred it to my brain.

My husband can sing anything that he has once heard. As a child, some nun, long lost in his memory, taught him to read music by do-re-mi's. He can pick up an unknown song and sing it by note. I still cannot!

# Thirty-Five

## OH, THE SOLACE OF NATURE!

Besides art, I found great solace in nature during these years. I taught science to the four upper grades. We did great things in our wide set-up of aquariums and terrariums.

One lady set up a very expensive tropical fish aquarium for us. I went in, the first night, with a flashlight, to check on them. I almost fainted. They all looked dead! Did you know that some fish go to the bottom at night and sleep on their sides? I didn't!

We had terrariums with beautiful moss and swamp plants like the tubular insect plants. These plants have a decadent odor. They are also lined with hairs pointing downward. In the wild, they collect rainwater. Because of the odor, insects are attracted. They go down and drown in the water. That is the plant's way of getting nitrogen, as it grows in bogs, and its roots can't reach soil.

We'd let a bunch of bugs in at the end of the terrarium opposite the plant. They would trot right over and march down to their death! Even if they changed their minds, they couldn't crawl back out, because those hairs that made such a smooth slide down now prevented them from crawling back up! One huge Cecropia caterpillar tried to get inside. It was too big, so it settled for making a large cocoon over the top of the plant.

Every night the orb spider eats its web. They make a new one every day. Their bite paralyzes their victim. They wrap them like a mummy, to keep them quiet while they suck out the juices.

This is the web of an orb spider. Notice the spider in the middle. Only the female makes a large web.

We had our very favorite big black and yellow Orb spider. The female makes that perfectly round, perfectly gorgeous web. We watched as she did just what the World Book Encyclopedia said spiders do. She chewed or sucked on each of her eight legs, oiling them so that she could scoot over her web without sticking. Then she sat in the middle of her web. We'd let a fly or grasshopper in, and like a bullet, she was on them weaving silk from her spinneret, to encase and immobilize them like a mummy. Every night she'd eat her web, and in the morning there'd be a new one in a different corner. We sure loved that spider! (Note: She really was dangerous. I don't advocate anyone playing with spiders. I don't like them myself. Without due care, she could have harmed us as well as her prey.) It was just that she was such an educational wonder.

The eighth grade boys from the other classroom wanted to borrow her and feed her, one noon. Someone got the bright idea to drop her down the stairwell, thinking that she'd swing on a web. Instead, she splattered on the step.

I tore into the classroom yelling through my tears and demanded they find me another one. They did, several, but they were all males, and males don't make webs. End of Spider Chapter.

The boys used to bring snakes for the terrariums. They had to be under a foot long. To make the other teachers satisfied that no snakes got into their rooms, our terrariums were quite well sealed. They were balanced. The plants provided oxygen for the animals. The animals provided fertilizer and carbon dioxide for the plants. There were plenty of earthworms in the soil of each terrarium. Any reptile or amphibian that can live in a terrarium will eat earthworms. We had a real good system going. Even the snakes liked the insect plants. They'd crawl in there to sleep. When we'd come into the classroom in the morning, it was not unusual to see snakes peeking out of the pitchers of the plants.

One day a seventh grader begged to take our emerald green-backed, yellow-bellied grass snake to his classroom. I said, "You promise not to get me in trouble!"

"Oh, no, 'Ster," he says.

Well, he immediately got in trouble and his teacher said, "Give me that."

"No, please, 'Ster. I'll put it in my desk and not take it out again!"

It came time to go to mid-morning Mass and he couldn't, or wouldn't, leave his buddy behind. He was putting his friend in his pocket to take, so it could worship its God in church, and Sister reached out and said, "Sorry, I warned you." Now she had never touched a snake and it never entered her mind that it was real. I myself thought it was fake when I first saw it.

It was a quiet little snake until she dropped it into her desk drawer. She screamed and almost fainted as said snake took off like a streak. Well, the lad retrieved my pet and I never became that nun's favorite acquaintance.

This was our graduation bulletin during my last year. All students interested were always invited to work on bulletin boards.

These just happen to be pictures that I still have of bulletin boards, done by students my last years of teaching.

This bulletin board was very 3-dimensional. The vines and plants were alive. Maybe you can still see Fujiyama's reflection in the lake. Mt. Fujiyama was made of tinfoil and spray painted brown. It had a white plaster tip of "snow." The real branches had apple blossoms of chalk-colored popcorn. The sprayed tinfoil land with holes cut to insert African violet plants was impressive!

I had gone to an Audubon camp before school started. It was in Spooner, Wisconsin. They had permission to net the Namekagon River for educational purposes. During the summer school year, they had an aquarium. We were the last group that summer. Somehow, I was given a huge plastic pail with all kinds of minnows.

The trip home took 4-5 hours. I blew air into the pail all the way home, to give air to the "fishies". They lived! Note my second long aquarium.

A month or so later, a man said to me, "Sister, do you know that you have a baby sturgeon in here?"

"Yikes! No I didn't know!" It acted like a vacuum cleaner sucking up debris! I don't remember what happened to the sturgeon. I do remember the other fish bullying it. I'd take a pencil with an eraser and hit them on the head when I saw them abusing it. Notice all terrariums and aquariums had lights. They were tightly contained as lizards, salamanders, and snakes would like to escape! The students provided the critters, some terrariums were sealed. They had earthworms, and other critters and plants. They were balanced and not opened for months. They were carbon dioxide and oxygen balanced. It was a great education even for me!

We had several kinds of salamanders; anything that can live in an aquarium can live on earthworms.

Notice the large long aquarium. We called it, "Our Lake Wisconsin." Our specialty was snakes. We had bright green grass snakes with yellow bellies, cinnamon with red bellies, gray De Kay snakes, pine snakes, and milk snakes. To qualify, they had to be less than 12 inches. Only one snake of a kind was allowed.

I think that I remember one of the children's dads taking the sturgeon minnow to Lake Winnebago to release it. He was probably dreaming of spearing it 30 years later!

One time we had a large aquarium harboring frogs' eggs. A lot had hatched into pollywogs. Someone brought in a beautiful large black salamander with raised yellow dots on its back. We put it in the aquarium. The rest of this story is tragic. If you're squeamish, don't read it.

The salamander was gorgeous. Their swim pattern is positively entertaining.

At recess we had 29 pollywogs. At noon we had 19. After the second recess, the salamander was belly-up and split wide open down its belly.

Lesson learned – after we quit crying was: in nature they probably wouldn't have access to so much food. Pollywogs would have been hiding under debris. Also either the pollywogs or frog eggs must have expanded. They were very small, having just hatched.

# Thirty-Six

## FINAL VOWS

Well, I've avoided the issue long enough. I was so unhappy that the inside of me thought that I would never smile again.

I was still cooking for ten or twelve people. This had now become an art and a definite solace. I was also teaching 50 eighth graders. I who had started out not knowing more than how to peel a potato, and crack an egg!

The nice thing about it was that I didn't have to do dishes. This is a lovely tradition that I carried into marriage! Let it never be said that I am stupid!

I decided that if going to a psychiatrist would help me save my vocation, I would ask permission to do that. I went once a week for over a year. Never was leaving the convent an issue.

About three years previous to this, I spent the summer preparing for Final Vows. Up to then, I had taken vows for one year, then two and lastly three years. We took vows for six years and had formation studies for three years before that.

As I recall at that time, years ago, we were taught that we had answered our vocation when we entered. It was to be assumed that that was our God-given vocation unless the Community informed us otherwise – that we were not suited to be a part of that Religious

Community. Now, some people are asked to leave! Some left of their own accord. The majority took their vows and lived as happily as anyone in any other walk of life.

But I had come so inexperienced and without a Catholic family foundation or support system. I'm sure the Sisters didn't understand this or I certainly could have been helped.

Before Final Vows, I explained my situation, as thoroughly as I knew how, to the Bishop's representative. I told him of my background history as plain as I have in this book.

I said, "Father, I hate every aspect of this life. Do I have the <u>right</u> to take the vows?"

He said, "From what you've told me, and the Community has told me, you definitely have a vocation. It will be very, very difficult for you to live in this vocation. You must consider that seriously."

And I said, "Father, I didn't ask you if it would be difficult, I asked you if I had the right, because if I have the right to take the vows, I will!"

Woe is me! Can you believe my naïve stupidity? If I had told my superiors that, I'm sure they would have advised me to leave. However, it seemed to me to be God's will and as I look back, I still believe that it was. So I took Final Vows.

Well, anyway, I confided in my counselor. I fought with him, hated him, and respected him. He prescribed so much medication that I dared <u>him</u> to swallow all that crap and try to stand in front of a classroom and teach.

(Ramble) Now Obedience was not my favorite vow. But I practiced obedience to the very best of my capability – heck, I carried it later into marriage and obeyed my husband and my kids. I'm forever, sometimes ridiculously, jumping to someone else's tune. Some of this is reflective and some of it is deliberate.

When I had my Cortisone Party, I had lots of left over chips and dips. I saved some for my family but I begged people to take some home so that I wouldn't have too much. One of my sons called from college and said, "Ma! You didn't give that all away did you? I wanted it for the Packer playoff game for a party with my friends."

So I called people and said, "Hey, I have to have some of that back!"

"No problem," said the women. (Women understand stuff like this.)

All three of my family men, including the son who originally jumped me about it, said, "Ma! You didn't ask for food back! How could you?"

They just don't understand how involved I still am with Holy Obedience. It empties one of self. It's spiritually freeing. They probably think I'm nuts.

Poverty is truly a royal gem.

My husband and I practice the spirit of Franciscan Poverty every day – always will. Now granted, sometimes we think it's a necessity but truly it's just a beloved habit or free choice. St. Francis knew that Poverty, embraced, was a dear Sister!

Chastity. This never posed a real problem for me. I never longed for marriage. Never consciously thought of wanting a husband and family. My life was full of children.

This picture was taken in 1964. Notice St. Mary's of Crivitz. It had just been rebuilt after the old church burned down. Two of these sisters are deceased. Two left the Order. I am on the right.

Notice the new habit change. Soon after these sisters no longer wore habits. They also took back their original names. They could keep their religious name if they wished. I left the Convent a month after this picture was taken.

# Thirty-Seven

## THE DEFEAT CALLED DEPRESSION

In a Christian marriage, Chastity is a necessary building stone.

The crazy world that is driving itself into a universal insane asylum has sex and love confused. Sex is first and foremost in their minds and people wonder why they can't find love. <u>Love and respect</u> come first and foremost. Sex is to be a wholesome satisfying expression of that love.

Nobody admits it to talk about it, but believe or not, in everyone's life, at different times for different reasons, sex may be impossible. So then, what does the crazy world do? Learn to <u>love</u> or commit suicide?

Our videos and soap operas and movies would have us believe that sex is the only thing in life. Believe it or not, we do have other body parts that are vital to life. I just don't understand this crazy, insane rat race that people make out of sex. Apparently, it doesn't bring them happiness because as far as I can see or hear, the sexually insane world is miserable.

I woke up one morning at Summer School, three years after taking Final Vows, convinced that I simply could not go on. I know now that it wasn't the vows that defeated me. It was the baggage that I had brought along into a way of life that I couldn't adjust to. I still feel I gave it all I had.

Believe it or not, up until that morning (other than after my father's funeral), I never considered leaving. I thought God wanted me there and the only thing I wasn't willingly going to give Him was my sanity. In my depression, I thought that that was imminently in jeopardy.

My psychiatrist had once said, "You may leave the convent, but <u>you</u> will always be a nun." Now that was a helluva thing to say! I knew what he meant because I had bared my soul to him. In some ways, 45 years later, he's still right, and it's O.K.

At my last visit to him, he said, "You have shown no sign of mental illness. I'm surprised that you made this decision. However, the important thing for you to have done was to make a decision.

Just before school closed that spring, I had dismissed a class for recess. As I passed a large mirror in the empty hall, I caught a reflection of myself. The thought that came to me, scared me to the marrow of my bone. It was, "If somebody doesn't touch me pretty soon, I won't even know if I exist." Now even I knew that was a precarious thought!

Today, I've become a hugging, touching person. I pat people, threaten them with outlandish, preposterous proposals, all as a result of one time not really knowing if I existed, or if I would just disappear into a vapor!

# Thirty-Eight

## ISN'T THERE ANOTHER WAY?

*I* mentioned having gone to the psychiatrist previously. Remember all the medications? Well, they are given to break down one's inhibitions so that they talk. To my way of thinking, they opiate the mind so that you also don't know what you're saying. These drugs were responsible for my loss of appetite and weight loss.

Now if I was leaving the Convent, I certainly would have to be facing and speaking to authorities. I did not want them to be clear-headed and me off on Cloud Nine.

So I flushed five bottles of anti-depressants, sleeping pills, etc. down the toilet. That was not my wisest move. That is not the way the medical profession would advise weaning oneself from medication. As a result, my short-term memory got really shaken—I mean royally! If I'd gone fishing, I probably would have accidentally walked off the pier. If I'd have thrown an anchor overboard, I probably would have gone in with it.

Whatever part of the brain manages short term memory was mangled.

Actually, at the time of this writing, I'm going through much of the same thing. Both the high doses of Cortisone and the prescribed cutting down of the dosages, leave me forgetting what I was saying or doing. It's manageable but annoying – and what the heck! I know this territory! I went through it thirty years ago!

I made an issue of the ring that denoted my final vows. I obtained another ring to turn in when I left, because the one I wore was my Mother's wedding ring. Dad had paid eleven dollars in 1915 for this 14 carat gold ring. The subterfuge probably wasn't necessary, but I could not risk losing Mom's ring. She didn't need it back, as she had replaced hers with another one. To this day, I frequently wear this ring in place of my own diamond. It spans my mother's marriage, my years in the Convent, and the 45 years of my own marriage.

The Mother General received my request. She was stunned.

She said, "Sister, I've looked through all the records. I've talked to Sisters you've lived with. There is no hint that you were unhappy."

I said, "Mother, the hell was inside me. I didn't make it for other people."

She said, "Think about it. Can't this be changed in any way?"

I went upstairs and looked over my beloved Convent grounds, past that great garden, and out over the water. I loved that place! But I had gone through too much pain to think it ought to be wasted. I thought, "No matter what I'd do, within myself, I'd just wind up back here again. I'd have to face the same pain over, and this coward had had all the pain she could take.

I had had a powerful prayer experience the previous year. I was kneeling at the Stations of the Cross where Christ was stripped of His clothing. I had asked God once more to strip me of everything that was not Him, even if it meant leaving the Convent.

I knew that was feasible, if I were to ever find peace. At the time, it was a booming terrible possibility. I had been in the world and I hadn't found peace there before.

To me, the thought of leaving a life that I loved but apparently couldn't personally live, was tantamount to praying to God – take me! Car accident, sickness, lightning, whatever, but take me! It was so reminiscent of the time when I was eighteen and praying among the hazel bushes, that it was frightening. I honestly believe that I had a vocation to Religious Life. I think it was meant, (unknown to me) to prepare me for the single life and marriage.

I left the Convent and moved to Green Bay. Only at that time and at that place could I have met the man, whom I am convinced, God planned for me.

Only through Chet could I have had the sons who are so dear to me. Only through them could I have my beautiful daughter-in-laws and the five wonderful children who call me "Grandma"!

Religious Life prepared me for the Sacrament of Matrimony. Without that training, my marriage could never have been what it is. Thank you, God!

# Thirty-Nine

## MORE REMINISCING

Just like at writing about Dad's death and my last mission, I now need to divert the flow of thought to another direction for a while.

My Grandma was now in her late eighties. She had broken a hip and, therefore, the doctor refused to let my mother continue to live with and take care of her. So Grandma went to a nursing home where my sister was an assistant administrator. Grandma died at age ninety-four.

Recently, I was very captivated by a special in Newsweek magazine. It was about the changes that have taken place in the last one-hundred years. Everything mentioned was a beating, pulsing memory within me.

Having been raised basically as an only child by aging parents, I came up with a sense of history. My parents' memories and stories and experiences were to me what movies, T.V., videos and computers are to today's youth.

My Grandfather's dad was a Civil War veteran. Grandpa had a bayonet and canteen that had belonged to his dad. I still have pictures of my great-grandfather in his Civil War uniform. It was a postcard with a note to Grandpa, signed, "Your soldier boy, Father."

At her death, my Grandmother distinctly remembered and

reminisced about the Wright Brothers and their three minute flight at Kitty Hawk. Grandma had grown up near Kitty Hawk. Wilbur Wright died in 1948, the year I went to the Convent.

Two years before Grandma's death in 1968, John Glen took the first step on the moon. She watched very alertly as an astronaut bounced around its surface. My then-to-be husband and I watched a full moon one night, in awe, as we were out spooning on a lovers' lane. That night, on that same moon, men were out walking! (Strangely enough, we couldn't see them!)

In 1912, the unsinkable Titanic sunk. In the minds of both my parents, that was indelible. I later married a man whose uncle came over on the Carpathian when he was seventeen. Uncle had no money. But he was young and healthy and knew that he could work if he got to America. His old eyes lit up once when he told me how he lived during the trip on sausages he hid up above the log rafters of the hold! The World Book Encyclopedia says the Carpathian picked up 705 survivors that night. Uncle, traveling in the hold or not, was part of that!

Uncle was from Poland. As a young lad, he was escaping the poverty and oppression that was building in Europe. Six years later, he sent money to his sister to come to America. His sister became my husband's mother – my sons' grandmother.

History ties us all together and I fear that today – buried in speed, and change, we are losing a sense of history.

In 1914, World War I began in Austria.

My parents married in 1915.

In 1917, America entered the First World War.

My father's brother escaped death in the fierce battles in the Argonne Forest in 1918 in France.

In 1918 and 1919, the worst influenza epidemic in history swept our country. Over 500,000 American died. Mom and Dad both contracted it. Somehow, they kept it away from their three little children in that log cabin!

Mom lost a very dearly beloved brother and sister to that

epidemic. One of those was buried without ever knowing that her brother had died, and was buried before her. Mom could not attend the funeral because she was fighting the virus.

I just checked World Book again. When my oldest son was four years old, I was simply compelled inside to get a set of World Book Encyclopedias! Grandpa's blood runs in my veins! Now my set is old. My kids laugh at it; "Good heavens, Ma, its copyright 1978!"

Well, sons, I'm old. Most of my life is in the past. When you have children, tradition in this family should lead you to buy an updated printing. If you're wise, you'll keep yours updated. Considering the speed with which knowledge and events unfold today, you will have to update yearly!

Now as I look back at this, I realize there are no book encyclopedias. They're all on the internet.

Thomas Edison died in 1931. He was a major part of the changes that took place in my lifetime. We had no electricity. Electricity at the time was new and novel. It was comparable to computers ten years ago.

Remember, I was not a Catholic at this time. No one in my family was. I'll always remember that one day, when I was five. My father rose from his chair by the radio and for some reason that I've never forgotten, declared, "There's white smoke over the Vatican!" Now How's that, folks? Pope Benedict XV had died and the Cardinals had elected Pius XII. Now wouldn't my Solemn Communion teacher have loved me if I had told her that? I didn't know what it meant at the time but it has been imbedded in my memory for fifty-nine years!

We had kerosene lights in each room. Near Dad's chair, where he read at night, was a gasoline lantern with gauze mantles that illuminated when the lantern was lit. Next to that was our "modern pride and joy." We owned a radio! It was only played for news.

It was World War II time. History books don't succeed in telling us how really terrible this was. World War I had ended only twenty years before! My Mother and Dad had two sons in World War II – my brothers! You better believe we listened to the news! Every word of the daily newspaper was absorbed and discussed avidly by the three of us. Red barely missed being killed in action. Just before the Allies and Russians met at the Elbe River, he was shot. The shrapnel went through his left ear and out the right side of his neck, barely missing his spinal cord.

As I recall the story, a German Medic carried him to an American Red Cross station, and then surrendered. A priest came to give Roger the last Sacraments, because his dog tag said, R.C., meaning Roman Catholic. Roger hadn't known what to put down when they asked his religion and decided to go with what he thought was Dad's religion. After our Baptisms, my Mom sent him instructions in the mail through the Knights of Columbus. Even later, he met a wonderful Catholic woman who became his wife.

Back to our radio. Besides the news we'd listen to "Fibber McGee and Molly" and "Amos and Andy." There was a great band we used to listen to. The director was imprisoned for sending secret U.S. intelligence messages to the Germans through some code in his music. His first name, to the best of my memory, was Heini. It was great music but America was shocked and awakened by the portentous possibilities of his schematic entertainment.

We were rich. Our World War I Veteran uncle was really rich! He had piles and piles of wonderful magazines that we inherited monthly. We were rich in life and in Norman Rockwell; -- in Reader's Digests, Outdoor Life's, Sports Afield, Life, Look, and National Geographic's. If that's not wealth, tell me what is!

Besides my mother was librarian of the local Women's Club. Every two months, we'd get big boxes of new books from the State Library. She even let me read Grapes of Wrath when it first came out. Great woman that she was, she clipped together pages that I shouldn't read because they were too sexually graphic. "Ya, Ma!"

Even when I had gone back to the Convent the second time, I had seen less movies than I could count on one hand. The books that I had read were innumerable.

The Dionne Quintuplets and I were born in the same year. They appeared on the scene six months before me. There was a lot of publicity about them. They were always shown in such cute poses and in such beautiful dresses. They were so rich, and I was so poor. Little did I or the rest of the world understand how really poor they were, and what a hell life was to be for them. It still saddens me, as the remaining survivors will forever suffer for the way they were raised and abused.

I grew up during the anxiety of building home bomb shelters. After all, the U.S. had just annihilated Nagasaki and Hiroshima. I also remember that postage stamps cost 3¢ - not the 49¢ of today! We didn't send many letters, back then because it cost <u>so much</u>! We just didn't have the money!

# Forty

## THE END OF A DREAM

So ten days after my request, we went to the Bishop's representative to sign the dispensation.

As I entered the room he said, "Sister, I see you have pushed it as far as you can!"

"Yes, Father, I have," was my response.

"You do realize that you can enter any Order, he said, except this one."

Now, that made me question whether I ought to sign the dispensation. If I ever wanted to enter an Order again, it would certainly have been this one. I have never felt any antagonism toward the Order, certain nuns maybe, myself in relation to them and it, but not the Order.

So the Bishop's representative closed the interview with this statement. "You do not owe the Church or Convent anything. The Church or Convent does not owe you anything."

Now, it had never entered my mind that anyone owed anyone anything. At one time, historically, certain Orders or the Church imposed penances, such as daily required prayer or charitable community service, as a penance for leaving the vow. Those days were past.

I also knew that this statement was meant to protect both the Convent and me from possible litigation.

However, that statement hit me like a rock in the pit of my stomach – or soul. It was like dumping a boulder into a lake and there it sat at the mucky bottom always visible to me. Something about it just wasn't right. By now, I wanted out, and out quickly, so there seemed to be nothing to discuss.

All told, I had spent fourteen years in the Convent. I had been born and raised in poverty, (and it only made me rich). I had spent fourteen years living the spirit of Poverty, (and I became richer). But facing me, without anyone's real knowledge, was raw, naked poverty and it was a little more than I thought I might be able to handle.

I had come with a hundred-dollar dowry. This was returned to me. I had some material, for dresses, from the Community sewing supplies. Normally, there would have been a good selection. The materials were odds and ends of bolts that a Sister obtained from a factory in Milwaukee. However, several women had left the Convent before me and had cleaned out anything that was appropriate to make into street wear.

This same Sister had shopped with me in Milwaukee. I also had a pair of shoes and three house-dresses. This was in 1966. Two of the dresses cost $7.99 apiece. The really pretty one, that I wore only once, because it really was inappropriate, cost $10.99.

I was going back into the world almost as naked as I was when I was born almost thirty-three years before. Only I knew how naked and empty and sick I was.

Once again, like at birth, I couldn't eat. Food looked and smelled good but at the sight of a plateful, I stopped dead. Actually, the prescription I had been on earlier had made me immediately anorexic.

Well I guess if this book is to be finished, I must go on. The Sisters drove me back to the home of the priest who had helped me enter the Convent. My Mother had gone to stay with him and his sister for several days while I was there.

I know that this seems to be an abrupt ending – but that's how it was for me – torturously abrupt.

My book has been divided into three parts. I hope you've enjoyed the read as much as I have enjoyed living most of it! God bless you!

# Forty-One

## FROM CHRYSALIS TO COCOON

I had been a nun. I left the Bay Settlement Convent on August 12, 1966.

The nuns had taken me to Neva, WI where I spent three days with my former Pastor, Father Hubert. His sister Bea and my mother were also there.

During my three day stay at Neva, a friend came and brought many fashionable clothing outfits for me.

I weighed 130 pounds. At five feet seven inches any size 12 fit beautifully.

This friend provided me shelter until she and her husband could renovate a building that was condemned. They made very fine living quarters out of this old home. This was rented to my Mother and me at a very minimal cost.

There were two Good Samaritans in my life. One was my mother, who in her aging years did everything that she was capable of in order to help me.

Another was the friend who offered tremendous love and support. Time and circumstances have separated us. I have always loved and prayed for her.

I know that I could never repay this friend, nor would she have accepted it, if I could have. However, I have tried to help others along the way, as the years passed, in the manner in which she helped me. I always told those "others" that I had a debt to pay and if they felt obligated to me, to pass the love and gifts on to someone else who was in need, when they themselves were enabled to be givers.

In talking with other people who have left religious life, I realize that we've shared some common dilemmas. People who want to help often tend to help too much. They seem to usurp the new found freedom of the fledgling lay person. This causes a tension not understood by the friend.

Remember the nun that looked into a mirror and wondered if she existed? Well, now I knew that I existed. Every mirror reflected beauty and I wished that I <u>didn't</u> exist! I couldn't face it. Here was a body, dressed to kill – even modestly humble clothes couldn't hide the life and beauty. But beauty and emptiness leave a hell of their own. My soul was torn and shredded and empty.

There were many issues that needed looking at, needed counseling, needed closure. But life had to go on immediately.

What reflected back from the mirrors now was like an empty Monarch butterfly chrysalis after the butterfly has hatched and flown away.

Maybe others didn't realize it, but I was totally aware of the plastic-covered emptiness of that chrysalis, that <u>everyone including</u> myself should have seen was empty. There were still little gold dots on it to remind me of the spiritual beauty that had been, but the life inside was gone – to where – only God knew.

In order to handle the tensions and the totally foreign new world that I was facing, I had to have an armor of protection. I built, not a transparent chrysalis, but an opaque cocoon. Around me, I shoved everything, that I could not face squarely, and handle, inside of that large grey cocoon of my sub-conscious.

Now a cocoon is airtight and waterproof. It's sealed tightly until the life within goes through a complete metamorphosis. All the cells give up their individuality, although keeping their own genetic make-up. When these cells rearrange into a new and glorious creature, it opens the cocoon; and the new, but essentially the same being within, takes wings and claims the air.

I left the Convent at almost thirty-two years of age. I just subtracted to see how many years ago that was. It was almost thirty-two years since I left.

## Forty-Two

## LOOKING BACK ON EDUCATION

In the 50's and 60's, I was a Bay Settlement Franciscan nun. We were a Diocesan order under the Auspices of the Bishop.

The number of schools we served really burgeoned the convent's supply of teachers. Second year novices who should have been being educated were often sent out to teach. They were guided by their supervisors.

Apparently I was judged to be a good teacher. My college education was obtained during summer school and night school at St. Norbert's in De Pere.

I loved teaching – anywhere – any age.

There were almost no lay teachers at the time. Salaries were so low that lay people found it prohibitive to volunteer!

I remember that the book bills on my first mission were $26.00 per student. Parishioners paid no tuition.

Nuns, at the time were given $50.00 a month. This was used for their mission needs. The excess was sent to the Mother house to help care for the elderly and disabled.

I've experienced highly educated teachers in college and elsewhere who were poor educators, I've seen nuns with minimal education who were terrific teachers. They understood and emphasized with students' minds in the learning practice.

Teaching and prayer were basically our lives. We had the time and opportunity to become great teachers. It didn't always turn out that way but the challenge was there!

We were unlike public school teachers for whom it was a job, no matter how dedicated they were. They had spouses, children, and pets and another whole environment to manage after school hours.

We had the opportunity for easier excellence. Most of the education I did have in no way prepared me for entering the marvelous world called CHILD – let alone 50 children more or less.

The least number of students I ever had was 34; I almost always had two grades.

The only time that I had one grade were the three years, at St. Jude's in Green Bay, when I had 48 students. At the same time, I was head cook for 10-12 nuns.

I started my school year by explaining that each student knew more about many topics or hobbies than I did. I was a <u>leader</u>.

Considering that I acknowledged that they all knew much more than me in many areas, none of them had to prove that!

Therefore, I guided, they contributed, and we learned together.

During this time, I taught 5$^{th}$-8$^{th}$ grade science. We always had aquariums and terrariums. The boys liked that they could bring almost anything to school, if it fit the subject. Therefore the boys liked me. Somehow in that equation it translated to, "if the boys like you, so do the girls because anything the boys like at that age – so do the girls. I think we fit well together! Fifty years later, I still love those kids!

# Forty-Three

## SEARCHING FOR A JOB

*I* did not want to teach in a Catholic school, mainly because I needed to start a new life away from nuns.

My priest friend had offered to send me for Montessori training but in between, he wanted me to set up school in his parish. At this time, I did not want a lengthy commitment to anyone or anything.

I thought I'd like to be a baker, but it was night work, and I had no car nor did I drive.

I applied to be a dentist's assistant. This dentist was very interested as he had a sister who was a nun. He was willing to train me but a very qualified experienced assistant applied after I did. He was forced by common sense to hire her.

My own sisters had all done waitress work. I applied for a hostess position in a supper club. The owner said, "No way, I was a seminarian and I had a breakdown coming into my father's business. I simply could not subject you to this environment, right out of the Convent. You'd crack up!"

I had thrown away all my teaching outlines, artwork, and props, before I left the Convent. I didn't envision or desire to go back into the same environment. Had I given those items to my Sister friends, I could have asked to have them back. Instead, I had put them in the incinerator.

At the prospect of leaving the Convent, I was painfully aware of the need to cut all the things that could possibly keep me attached. I knew that I needed freedom. I needed to cut the umbilical cord that connected me to Religious Life.

I asked the nuns, even my best friends, never to contact me. I, in turn, intended not to contact them. Tearfully, my friends and I agreed.

However, this was of short duration. Three weeks later I had to attend a Diocesan teacher's convention. We were all rejoicing over the fact that we had all survived the ordeal of my leaving.

One night, two weeks after I left the Convent, a priest called me. He said, I'm told that you are a good teacher. I've sent several messages your way and people tell me that you refuse to consider teaching again. Well, I have a classroom of fifth and sixth grade students coming in tomorrow and I have no teacher! Will you please take the job?" This was at St. John the Evangelist in Green Bay.

It certainly seemed to me that God was moving the checkers again. I told Father how I felt. It was agreed upon that I did not have to attend daily Mass unless I so desired. I did not know any of the nuns at the school as they were not from the Order to which I had belonged. I did not have to worry about attachment.

My contract said that no nun was to contact or approach me about anything unless I made the first move. To their credit, they abided by the contract.

During the second week of school, great sadness once again struck. One of my sisters died after a long struggle with many illnesses. She was fifty years old. She left a husband and two pre-adolescent children.

At the end of the year, when I was comfortably visiting with my fellow teachers one of the nuns said, "You have no idea how many times I wanted to just put my arms around you and hug you!"

I have always been loved. Looking back upon my personal history, I know that I have been much luckier or blessed than many people whom I've known. I have never been abused in any way by anyone. I surmise that my psyche could not have survived that.

There was quite a length of time when I was in the Convent that my whole being was convinced that no one "knew" me, loved me, or cared about me, -- probably even including God, in my mind, at times. I emphasize this to make a very powerful point.

We can be surrounded by, supported by, and blanketed in love. If we close our hearts or block off our minds and emotions, that love energy might as well be dripping onto a rock. It may finally get through, but for love to erode a heart of stone, takes a long time. If one <u>really</u> wants wholesome love, it is a lot easier to remove our own stone, even if just a little bit at a time, and let our hungry heart soak in the warmth and fertility of love – which after all, begins in the God who became Love Incarnate.

We perhaps think that any effort on our part to move our stone might be very painful. I can tell you from experience, nothing is as painful as the hell of isolation!

Let me reiterate. The Love of God is always there. The love of our fellow humans frequently is a constant. If we move outside the pull of force, the choice has been ours.

We have all been invited to the Party – here on earth and in Eternity. To be present or not is our choice.

# Forty-Four

## PERSONAL STRUGGLES

    I tried to dissolve that rock in the pit of my stomach with what little drugs I had at my disposal. I still had prescriptions that I had never had filled. I called a good Catholic friend once when both my mind and speech, and soul, were slurred. She accused me of being a drug addict. In her mind, that was the plain and simple truth. To her, medical prescriptions and illegal drugs, taken as opiates, were one and the same, <u>and they are</u>.

    In my mind, to this day, the plain and simple truth was that she left me bleeding alongside of the road, like the wounded, beaten traveler of the Gospels. She thought she was a good Catholic Christian, but she was definitely not a Good Samaritan.

    When I wasn't teaching, I'd take a pill and go to sleep. After hours of this, my Mother would say, "Why don't you wake up and we'll eat a while!"

    Well, gradually, I replaced the pills with food. It was quite a conscious substitution on my part. It started a life battle; one, which so far, I always lose. Food became my drug of choice.

    When men I dated, and particularly my husband, have ever made a comment about weight, I feel my feet plant firmly on the ground.

    First of all, the weight I put on anchored me to earth. An empty chrysalis blows around completely at the mercy of the slightest breeze. Crazy as this may seem, food and fat added substance to my perceived emptiness.

In our country, we are extremely weight conscious. To be thin is equated as beauty; I couldn't handle beauty.

Until after I was married, I only put on twenty pounds. The battle to eliminate these twenty pounds was equal to what I've fought since, to conquer the added two hundred pounds.

Also involved in this issue is always, "Do you really love me? Do you love me for who I am, or for what I do or don't do?

The world discriminates against obese people. We, discriminate in return. We dare the world to deny us the right to eat and breathe.

It's not a pretty fight and believe me; most of us would rather not be on the battleground. I'm hoping that when the subconscious within me comes pouring out freely, as a result of the high dosage of cortisone, it will have another result.

I know that weight loss is basically out of my control. I love to cook and I'm a compulsive eater. The eating problem started when I stuffed my subconscious closet. The door is now wide open; the closet is clean, and I hope the eating compulsion also goes away. At least, I'm now willing to give it a helping hand.

School went well. My personal life did not. I was consumed for weeks by deep interior urges seeming to demand fulfillment. This led to a terrible weight of guilt. I spoke to a confessor who, in the Sacrament of Penance, explained to me that what I had experienced was really not sexual sin, but rather, sin that was self-abusive and self-destructive.

I thank God that this cross was of short duration. It was hell – period. It did, however, open my eyes to the temptations and accompanying torture that many people face. Some are driven to insanity and worse because there is no one in their lives to guide them and help them understand themselves.

These last two paragraphs have been hard to write. Many human beings do have experience with this lonely self-destructive behavior and some of them hide their heads and die lonely deaths inside.

I felt compelled to write this. I have never spoken to anyone about this in all the years that have passed. I feel that it may be of help to some reader to understand that there is light and peace ahead. We, Christians, and particularly Catholics, in what is now called the Sacrament of Reconciliation, no longer need to get hopelessly caught in the centrifugal force of this vacuum.

Having stuffed so much into my subconscious, I felt that I had an immovable boulder in the pit of my stomach.

To this day, I have to admit that the intense upheaval in my soul in transferring from Religious Life to single vocation was a terrible adjustment to make.

There actually was no transition. It was like I had bungee jumped from a cliff to the rocks below. Even that's a poor comparison. With bungee jumping there's bouncing up and down. In this case, it was more like ker-splat! Get up, catch your breath and run!

# Forty-Five

## ENTERING THE WORLD OF MEN

Marriage and family were never a desire or felt need for me when I was in the Convent.

Now that my life had changed, I clearly had no intention to stay single. I had come home in August. At Christmas, I went out socially by myself for the first time. It was a Catholic singles dinner and dance. By February, my social calendar was as full as I could have wanted it to be.

Father Lord was a great teenage writer and adviser of the times. I used his advice often in talking with youth. Now, I was in their shoes and I tried to follow his advice. One important item was dating numerous partners so as to get acquainted with different personalities.

Now this was not the norm in the adult dating scene. But, I innocently did not know that. Neither did I know that the women in the group didn't like each other very much and liked former nuns even less. Competition was not welcomed with open arms and those former nuns presented a problem. They all seemed to know what they wanted and it was spelled MAN. We were all older and if we wanted marriage and a family, we needed to plan our strategy. Hopefully, it was on a straight path and forward!

One man taught me to dance. He was a wonderful ballroom dancer. One wined and dined me; one was just plain fun. One liked movies; one just liked to spend time with this woman who found everything exciting. Now instead of sleeping and eating, when I wasn't teaching, I was sleeping and dating (but not in today's concept).

I was so naïve that one time when a man asked me out to a movie on Friday, I said, "I think Leon is going to ask me out that night." Now, I knew, by the look on his face, that he had never met that kind of response before!

This went on for at least a year. One didn't really like me – he just needed companionship. One liked me a great deal but I thought he was too old. One was fun but I didn't think he could support a family. One was too independent, etc. etc.

Besides, I was not about to fall in love. That would mean I was vulnerable and I was not up to being hurt ever, ever, ever!

Also, I thought, "If any of these men really want to stop me from going out with the others, it's their move!" For now, I'm having fun!

They all knew I was playing the field.

There was one very handsome man in the group that all the girls buzzed about and, I thought, brazenly chased.

Because I didn't drive, other girls picked me up to go places when I first joined the singles' group. Chet came into their conversation often.

One lady said, "Chet is the only man in the group that I am interested in and he obviously isn't interested in me!"

My thoughts were, "Well, I certainly won't join those chasing him"!

# Forty-Six

## MEETING CHET

Chet was an officer of the group. One time he suggested changing some decorations for a party and I obediently changed them. He suggested someone should bake a cake for the group's anniversary. The next week, I obediently baked a huge cake. He winked at me and gave me the O.K. sign that my cake was good.

The singles group used to have a Thanksgiving supper. The girls all made food to bring. The guys actually checked to see who made food from scratch; whose mothers made the food, etc.

Gradually, some of the men I went with would question me, "Would you ever go out with Chet?" My answer would be, "Who wants to know? If Chet wants to go out, tell him to ask!"

Well, Chet was that good-looking guy. By now, I had decided he was a stuck-up – a run-around, (must be – the girls all chased him; every time I saw him). He'd come and help set up an event and leave. Therefore, I figured he was stuck up! Actually, he would go back home to take care of his mother who was dying of cancer.

I was elected an officer of the singles' group. Chet called me and said he'd pick me up for the meeting. Strangely enough, it became a lifetime pick-up, or I became a lifetime Pick-up! He said, "I knew that I was going to marry you the first time that I saw you, but I wouldn't cut in as long as you were going out with those other fellows."

His reason for being serious with me was that he knew I had been a nun. In his words, "You haven't wasted your life on yourself." Don't tell me God wasn't involved in this!

Chet and I dated three or four times a week for a year and a half. He and I had a shared hang-up. Neither one of us wanted to get hurt. Neither of us let down our reserve enough to know either infatuation or unconditional love. I measured and weighed his character, reliability, and financial status. Chet was orderly, disciplined, religious, and stable. To this day, I'm like a helium balloon on a string, anchored by his stability. I thank God always for that.

Raymond and his wife, Jean, had been close friends of mine for years. Jean and I were teachers together at St. Boniface in De Pere. I had taught and loved their twin sons in 6$^{th}$ grade.

My mother and I had enjoyed a meal and spent several evenings with them after I left the Convent. Raymond was an engineer for North Western Railroads.

Jean died suddenly of a heart attack. Many months later Raymond would bring the train in and stop by our house which was close to the train station.

I thought he needed understanding and solace. My mother knew long before I did, that he was courting me. I always told Chet when Raymond came to visit; I had no reason not to.

One night after Chet and I had gone to pre-marital instructions, I asked him, Chet, "Do you love me the way you'd want to love your wife?"

He turned to me with tears in his eyes and said, "I don't know!"

My exact thoughts were, "You 'son of a bitch'," I've given you a year and a half of my life, and you don't know if you love me the way you'd want to love your wife?" I left his house for good.

Either in spite, or on the rebound, Chet started dating a friend of mine, also a former nun. He had met her through me.

So now, Raymond saw his opportunity and made his move. I really fell in love. In a few short months, we had set a wedding date for August 10.

My Mom called my brother, from Atlanta, all excited. His wife coaxed a co-worker to change a European tour to another time so that she could come to the wedding.

Then one night I got a call from Chet, "Can I talk to you?"

# Forty-Seven

## ROMANTIC CONFUSION

"Well sure, everyone has a right to be heard," I thought. We went out and "talked." I'd done my duty. I wasn't swayed, and I thought that was that!

In the meantime, Chet made a vital move. He started going to daily Mass and talking to God non-stop, saying God had told him to fight for what he wanted. He said he had lost other battles in his life and this one he was going to win.

Well, I thought he'd started fighting this battle too late. One night Ray dropped me off, where I bowled in a single women's league. To be honest, I should say, "I tried to bowl." There really were worse bowlers in that league, but that didn't hide the fact that I was lousy.

Halfway through the frames, in walked Chet. He was one handsome specimen, dressed in his suit from the office. I still think he had too much brandy. Privately, he tells me he didn't have any. (He lies.) Publicly, the few times it's ever been mentioned, he claims he was drunker than a skunk. (He still lies!)

There in the middle of that crowded bowling alley, Chet knelt down and proposed, "Let's go out of state tonight and get married!" (He'll deny this!) But you recall I have a photographic memory of words and events.

"Problem number one – Ray just walked in; he's by the door!"

Chet got up and respectfully addressed Ray. I didn't hear Chet but Ray told me that it went like this:

"You've <u>had</u> a wife. I'm really sorry that she died. This woman is mine! You'd always expect her to be like your wife and replace her. With me, she could just be herself."

Ray said, "Well, I brought her here, and it's my responsibility to take her home."

I left in the car with Raymond. Chet turned his car and went in the other direction. No words could describe the tearing apart, right down the middle that took place in me. If I hadn't been such a coward, I would have jumped out of the car I was in and killed myself, just to avoid the conflict. I, who will avoid a conflict in any way possible, was caught right in the center of a screamingly painful rip.

I remember that Raymond was very quiet; however he did say that Chet was a fine young man. He was very impressed with him. He also said that he knew I was still in love with Chet.

It was very hard on Raymond because he had lost his wife suddenly in his arms and there was nothing he could do about it.

He felt that I had slipped away from him and once more he could do nothing about it.

I loved Raymond and I had a very high respect for him but my heart seemed to tell me to listen to my head!

I didn't tell my mother what was going on, but she had to know that I was devastated. I followed my usual tactics and escaped. Mom and I went to visit relatives. We stayed at the home of Ray, my brother-in-law.

He was the husband of my sister who had died the year before. Ray had not dated since my sister died. He said he could have used his money on wine and women but, up to that time, he had not dated. I was the first woman he took out since his wife's death. He had known and liked me for years and had liked all of our family.

He expressed his desire to have me move near his area and teach so that we could get better acquainted. In short, loud and clear, his proposal was marriage!

Now, that's just what I needed at the moment! I had escaped to that area for peace and the Houdinian knots got tighter and more complicated. Once again, this was a fine man!

One night I waited 'til almost 1:00 am. I kept dialing Chet's number and he was out. Believe it or not, he was on a date with my friend! How dare he keep playing around with a girl while I was entangled with other men?

He said, "Hello," and I heard my quavering voice say, "Can we talk? Now, he says it's my fault that we've been stuck with each other the last 45 years! I should have left well-enough alone! – He says:

We each had to extricate ourselves from a date the next night, but talk we did!

Believe it or not, this next story really happened. Several weeks earlier, when Ray and I had decided to get married, he had gone to visit Mom and asked her permission to marry me. She had given it.

Now she received a letter from Ray 2, my brother-in-law, declaring his intentions and asking her blessing.

A few days later, Chet called her and said, "I love your daughter. I will take good care of her. May I have your blessing and permission to marry her?"

My mother said, "Good God, I wish one of you would!"

In the meantime, the man who had been so much fun to date stopped by for old times to visit Mom. She was unloading her burdens on him.

He said, "You mean she's still up for grabs? I think I'll throw my hat into the ring!

Mom said "If you do, I'll kill you with my own bare hands!"

Chet proposed and I said, "Yes!"

Mom called my brother to tell them that the wedding date was changed to July 26th. My sister-in-law moaned, "Oh God, she didn't change the date?" They wouldn't be able to change plans to come on that date.

Mom yelled into their ears, "She not only changed the date! She changed the man!"

That needed a lot of explaining to a lot of people. I guess it kept my seventy-seven year old Mom young at heart. Well, maybe it aged her! Anyway it happened, and the decision has been for the better every day of my life since.

My beloved Chet had some explaining to do before he got that "Yes."

Get this, does this sound like an accountant's mentality?

"How did I know if I loved you the way I'd want to love a wife? I'd never had a wife!"

And the beaut' of all beauts' – "I didn't want to make a mistake that I'd regret <u>thirty</u> years later!! My love grows!"

## Forty-Eight

## MY LOVE GROWS!

So that was the theme banner of our wedding. *My Love Grows*.

Now the romantic part of my girlish heart did <u>not want</u> a love that had to grow! I wanted someone to be <u>smitten</u> with me; head over heels in love with me. Actually, the romantic part of me would still like that. But, you know what?

I've seen a lot of marriages that started out "head over heels" in love and they bit the dust years ago. My husband and I love each other zillions of times more now than the day we married. That love truly did grow, day by day, over rough roads and smooth. I wouldn't trade it for anything on earth! My mom and I had shopped for a positively beautiful wedding gown and veil. After we chose it, they gave us a wedding magazine that had that gown on the cover! Mom insisted on paying for it.

My girlfriend, Doris, and her boyfriend, Bob, were one couple. The other couple who stood up for us was my sister, Helen, and her husband, Eric Henkel.

The girls' long gowns were a beautiful yellow that could be cut off later for street wear.

The men, of course, were in tuxedos. Chet certainly was one handsome dude! I'm still astonished considering the girls who were after him, that he became mine! Even at our wedding, one girl was vocally astonished that he married me!

Our wedding was perfect. It was a beautiful day. All the confusion was cleared and there was only peace on the horizon. The wedding was held at St. Mary's of the Angels Parish in Green Bay, Wisconsin.

I had made 12 huge bouquets of dried items for bouquets in the basement. They were made with many sprays of sea oats and dozens of large dried thistle heads, sprayed different colors.

The members of Xavier Guild Singles Group made beautiful yellow-twisted crepe paper hangings the night before on the ceilings.

A family style chicken dinner was served for about 200 people.

Many of my students were at the Wedding Mass. Probably forty nuns attended. I have a beautiful photograph with about twenty nuns on it. The others left before dinner and weren't on the picture. There was also a lovely large picture of all the students who attended.

In the convent I was disturbed by the feeling that I just didn't fit. I was always studying others, and facing their reflection, I came up short. In married life, I have never had a moment of ambivalence. Here, I fit!

I've known many women who've gone through hell in marriage and motherhood. They've worked far harder to keep marriage going than I would ever dream of, yet their marriages have disintegrated and ended in divorce. Some have worried themselves sick since the day their children were born. Those same children have led them through hell and high water.

My attitude in marriage has been, "I'm doing the best I can. If that's not good enough - tough!" It boiled down to, "I'm tired of the proving game. If I have to prove my worth, to myself or someone else, the game is lost. Accept me as I am, see my worth, and love that." The battle cry has been, "Don't look for my faults. There's no challenge in that! I'm full of faults and they're very visible. If you want a challenge, find the good in me!"

At any rate, for me, marriage has only been a good. When I

squeeze my husband hard enough, he admits the same things! We both humbly thank God for this fact.

These are school pictures of me the two years that
I taught at St. John the Evangelist 1962-68.

# Forty-Nine

## THIS MAN IS NOT A FIGHTER

I've mentioned that I am not a fighter by nature. I did, however, know that I could quibble or argue with this man before I married him. Some men could certainly have inhibited me.

Early in our marriage, my husband and I had two fights. One, I thought, was really big. I wanted to go visit my relatives for the weekend and he did not. I had his car all packed. The argument became verbal, when he discovered that I hadn't packed his clothes. Now who'd have thought that a grown-up man couldn't round up his own wardrobe for a weekend?

As I recall, it ended up with my yelling at him and telling him how <u>he</u> thought that I was getting fat and lazy, and on and on and on! When I was all done, he quietly said, "Just remember who said that!!" That made me madder! I went out and unpacked his car and packed mine. He went out and unpacked my car and packed his. We went together but as I remember, I wished all weekend that one of us had stayed home with his originally unpacked clothes!

My husband says today that he doesn't remember that first fight. He never did catch on to the fact that there was a second fight!

I don't remember what that one was about. I just know that as I stood crying at the front window, watching him drive off to work, he didn't even know that we were supposed to be fighting!

I was so mad that I decided, then and there, to use my energy in a different way in the future. Since then, we've both tried to exert our efforts toward pulling together in the harness instead of each going a different way. Now I should have learned that as a child on the farm!

Actually, a team of harnessed horses pulling a wagon is not a bad simile for marriage. Quite a load can be pulled without undue exertion on either partner, if they are a well-matched team and are hitched and harnessed right. A good team barely needs a driver.

It's when one of the team balks and doesn't want to do its share that trouble begins. If one decides to race ahead or go a different direction, pain results. It's possible for a horse to break loose at great pain to itself and others. The bit tears the mouth. The eveners bang its heels bloody, but if confinement is too painful, the horse could fight against restraint and gain its freedom. It would surely injure its partner. The tongue of the wagon would probably break. Very likely, the wagon (of marriage), would tip and at least be damaged, if not smashed. Surely the occupants of the wagon (children) would be in grave danger or life-threatening harm.

All in all, it would be much less costly to plan and prepare and consider the cost involved, before hitching the wrong partners to any wagon, let alone a marriage.

Actually, my husband and I argue about many things. Some people might say that we do it all the time. But we argue about things. We have never turned those issues into personal vendettas like so many people do.

I know that my husband has never hurt me in anyway. One time when I wanted to check my own grasp of reality, I asked him if I had ever hurt him in any way. He gave me a usual man's answer, which meant he hadn't listened to the question! So, I pushed the issue and he said, "No, you've never hurt me. You've never come anywhere near it." Again, we humbly thank God!

It seems that writing about this part of my life takes effort. Living it was comparatively easy. I didn't stuff things into my subconscious in marriage, so reams of thoughts do not come pouring out onto paper. Besides, many of the nuns that I lived with are dead. The people in this part of my life are very much alive. They may well argue about every point they may read!

Steve was forever in the tulips.

Brother meets Brother

We are clowns!

Pete & Joe. Buddies I made for my sons.

TWISTED VINES – An Autobiography of an Ex-Nun

Mom made our buddies, Pete and Joe. They wore our old shoes and could stand up by themselves.

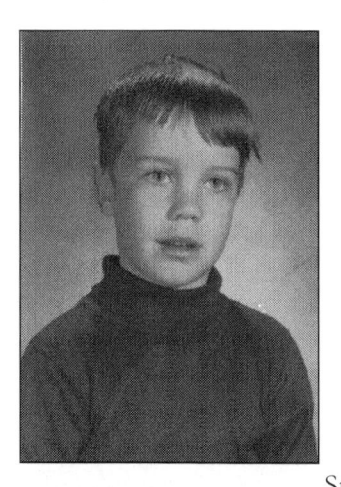

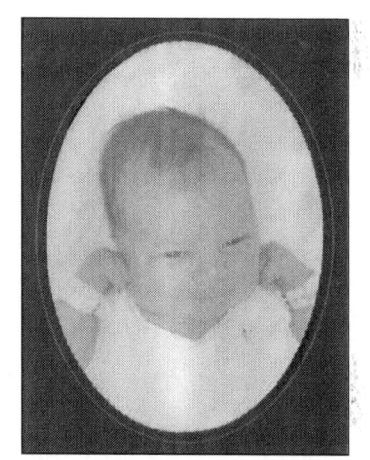

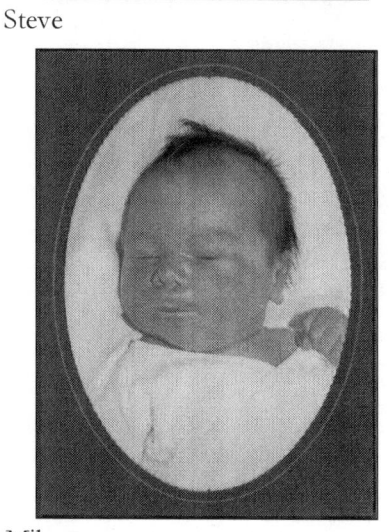

Steve

Mike

# Fifty

## THE PRIDE AND JOY OF MY LIFE

Two years after we were married, I finally became pregnant. Why I thought that I wanted a baby, I'll never know. I had only held a baby once or twice and had never changed a diaper. I was never attracted to other people's babies. If the kid had been born at age nine and over, I'd have been delighted! That stage I understood!

Pregnancy for me brought arthritis that never disappeared. Women in my dismissal-time, pre-natal classes would be getting into their cars outside and I'd still be standing by my chair trying to make believe that I didn't notice that my feet wouldn't move. Another great aspect of pregnancy for me was nine months of nausea and vomiting.

Not having watched movies or T.V. soap operas, I hadn't the slightest inkling of what labor and delivery was like – I can't imagine that any woman having gone through it would ever do it again. But, in time, I did.

I was thirty-seven when my first son, Stephen Joseph, was born. He had an RH negative blood type. As I understand it, my system, at the end of a very, very lengthy labor, was trying to do him in. I thought that he was trying to do me in! At any rate, he finally arrived on the scene weighing in at nine and a half pounds and measuring twenty-three and a half inches.

By the time I rested half a day and they brought this baby in to see me, he was the most gorgeous creation that I had ever laid eyes on. He was a blond, blue-eyed rosebud of humanity. He was then, and always has been, the pride of my life.

Raising this little guy was sheer joy. In his first six years, he was spanked only once. When that once came, I'm sure I could have been hauled off for child abuse.

His father had taken him out to the garden and wandered over to a neighbor's. My son was about two and a half and I was now pregnant for the second time. The little guy asked permission to ride a neighbor's tricycle. Son got permission; fathers kept talking. Son rode out into the street instead of turning down the sidewalk. Mother was talking on the phone, facing the street. It was getting dusk outside. I thought, "Do I see what I think I see? A child in the middle of the street?"

Just as I was becoming aware that the kid riding down the middle of the street was mine, cars passed him on both sides. I ran out, grabbed kid and tricycle, and spanked him all the way into the house to the tune of, "Don't you ever, ever, ever go on the street again!"

I changed his clothes for bed and at the sight of his little bare butt, I started spanking him again! It's a wonder that the poor kid ever learned to cross a street as he grew up.

My first son was almost three, when the second one arrived. This time my husband was present for the birth. We didn't plan it that way. Having dads present was new at the time. They were supposed to go to pre-natal classes and be approved, etc. We opted not to go that way because the first birth had been so hard.

Just before delivery, the nurse asked if my husband would be attending. I said that we hadn't planned on it.

She said, "I've witnessed many husbands during their wives' labor. If ever a man deserves to see his child born, this man does."

She conferred with the doctor who said, "Absolutely!"

It was wonderful to welcome son number two, together. He was an inch shorter than my first son but weighed the same, nine and a half pounds. His name is Michael John.

Today, some twenty odd years later, they're the same height, six feet, four inches.

I couldn't fathom loving another child as much as I did the first. That was a real concern. I loved the first one with all the love I had. Isn't it amazing how inclusive love is? Once he arrived, there was never a question.

I mentioned that my first son, Steve, is my pride. He is very much like his father.

My second son, Mike, is my joy. He is so much like me that all his life, when I'd be talking to him, I had the uncanny feeling that I was talking to myself. I often thought this is what I'd be like, if it weren't for my upbringing and background. Sometimes that's good, and sometimes that's bad. At any rate, my sons have always been my pride and my joy. I have much to thank them for.

My first son, Stephen, can never be thanked enough for how much he did to raise his brother.

I mentioned having all day sickness with my first pregnancy. By the second time around, I figured out that if I'd get up and get it over with, the rest of the day would be fairly good. One morning I was leaning over the basin, upchucking, when I noticed my first son making noises as he leaned over the wastebasket.

I said, "What are you doing?"

He answered, "I'm helping you upchuck, Mama!"

Son number two, Mike, decided to be a colicky baby. Bless his heart; he grew out of it before I flushed him down the pipes!

Running up and down the basement door at the cottage.

Mike by the tire swing. See Daddy's stump house in the back.
It was a lot of fun!

## Fifty-One

## WE BUY OUR OWN COTTAGE

When Mike was five months old; we rented a cottage for a week. A niece came along to help me take care of the baby.

It was quite a week. An uncle had brought a motor to my husband.

He said, "I've only used it seven times. I may never use it again. Take it!"

The large lake that we were on was shallow. With any kind of bad weather, it whipped up huge waves, making it impossible to go fishing. We had bad weather all week. After about the fourth day of that agitation, the men went to another lake. They stopped to ask some other men, who were building a cabin, for directions. These were very friendly men and a number of them came to chat for a while, at our car. About six miles down the road, someone noticed that the motor was no longer on the boat. Great searching turned up no motor and no oil marks on the road. Upon backtracking, there seemed to be no men building a cabin anymore that day, either! We think that they took the motor off the boat.

A bee stung Steve and he tended to react quite strongly to stings!

One noon Chet wanted me to go out and see where they were catching all the perch.

I threw out a small lure – sort of just playing, I thought I had a snag until the snag started moving. I was afraid and gave the pole to Chet.

A definitely legal musky, a real beaut, went under the boat to the other side and it was up, up, and away!

The men in our group were all casting big lures for musky – and I hooked one and let it get away!

The morning that we were to leave the cottage, we woke up to just a terrible odor. The owner's dog had tackled a skunk under the cottage. We had to throw all of our food away. All of our clothing had to be washed in order to get rid of the odor.

When we got home, I discovered that my car had been badly scratched from one end to the other. A brick on the corner of our home was broken.

I had loaned my car to a dear nun friend who was stationed in Nicaragua. She wasn't used to driving. It takes real skill to clear our house and pull into the right side of our garage. I had told Sister to leave the car on the driveway but it looked simple. She tried to put it away and got hung up.

The point is we had a horrible vacation.

A month later, my husband was out cleaning his tackle box and nursing his wounds. He had a vacation and nowhere to go!

I went out where he was, under the apple trees. I said, "Why don't you go to your sister's? You can fish and the kids and I will catch butterflies."

He retorted, "There are no fish in that damn lake!"

I said, "The lady whose husband died is selling her cottage."

Husband said, "So?"

I said, "So, two years ago when he died, you were interested in buying it!"

No answer.

Ten minutes later, the tackle box was all straightened out. Husband said, "You want to take a ride and look at that cottage?"

To make a long story short, by the next noon, the cottage was ours.

Husband said, "If you want this cottage, you can have it."

I didn't want to be blamed for this decision. I said, "I've never had anything. It's up to you. It's your money."

That wonderful husband of mine replied, "I've saved all my life for a wife and a family, and now I'm going to spend some of it!"

That's how we got the beautiful cottage on a spring-fed lake, which has made our life so different from many people that we know. Steve was three and a half and Mike was not yet one. They don't remember living without the cottage. It's part of the very warp and woof of their character.

I've always thought that the cottage made our children who they are. They were there every weekend. They bonded with nature. We almost always took friends along for company. By the time they were old enough not to want to go to the cottage every weekend because of friends and peers; they knew who they themselves were. They seemed to handle peer pressure quite well because of that stability within themselves.

As the boys were growing up, our real home was the cottage. I'd have the car packed with clothes and food when my husband came home from work. By 4:30 p.m., our car was headed north. We came home at 10:00 p.m. on Sunday night. The boys slept on the way home and Chet would bring them in and tuck them into bed. That was a fun game for them. He carried them in while they were playing "possum," long after they were big enough to have been substantial help unloading! I know that they thought they were pulling the wool over our eyes. Actually, they did! But we knew it, guys!

By the time I'd have the clothes washed, the house cleaned and more food prepared, it would be the end of the week and we were headed back to the cottage.

Each season is so special up north. In winter, my husband built a small snow hill by the back door. He shoveled and iced a path down the hill onto the lake. The kids could slide almost a full block from the doorway past the end of the dock. Hundreds of delightful hours were spent on "Otter Hill."

Our baby started ice fishing in his buggy, attached to a sled. Soon my family was out all over, skating over the lake. Ice fishing and skating clashed one beautiful day when Mike, at three, went over a partially drilled ice hole. Up went the skates, down went his butt. X-rays resulted in a cast on a broken elbow. Guess what? He skated and tobogganed the next weekend!

No fish in that lake – Hey Dad?

In the background is the original cottage appearance.

Otter hill went from the cottage way out past the end of where the dock was in summer.

Michael learned to love the outdoors early!

The spring hole
Mom broke through
while Dad was
fishing through
28' of ice nearby.
Notice the plastic
sled marks and the
boys' foot prints
right behind me.

## Fifty-Two

## THE FOUR SEASONS

There's a real mystique about ice fishing. You can sit in a boat in summer and catch the same kind of fish but there's never the thrill that you feel in winter. When a bobber bobs in that eight-inch hole in winter, your blood pressure rises. You watch that little bobber inch its way down the side of the ice and WHAMMO! Not until all the line is brought in, do you know what's on the end of that hook. The same type of bait might result in a bass, bluegill, perch, or trout.

We were always careful that the ice was thick enough to be safe. One time it was twenty-eight inches thick where my husband was fishing. I was pulling the boys, then three and six years old, around the lake on a sled.

All of a sudden, I had a strange sensation. My arms were straight out; water was up to my armpits, and I couldn't touch bottom with one foot. The other foot was on top of a stump.

The rope to the kids' toboggan was around my waist! The water would definitely have been over both of their heads.

I told them to roll, one at a time, toward the middle of the lake. Once that was accomplished, they were to run and get their father.

I was screaming and panicking, my boys were walking toward their father, who was probably four blocks away. I had hit a spring hole. The ice gave way just enough to let my body through. Where I went through, it was about a half-inch thick and honey-combed. The edges kept breaking, but eventually, I was able to get one leg out and then roll to safety. There must have been angels guarding me!

The boys ran back to me. I said, "Why were you walking? The oldest son said, "I had a wrinkle in my sock and it hurt."

Actually, I think they were afraid that with each new step, they might fall through! I explained that even if you were to bleed to death, you put pressure on the wound and go get help for someone who was drowning.

"Oh," said my oldest son.

We walked some distance in silence. Then he said, "I suppose I shouldn't say this, Mama, but you looked like a big orange bobber!" I had on a bright orange hunting jacket and hat. The silence was shattered by laughter.

No one could believe it could have happened. There were snowmobile tracks three feet for the edge of the hole! I didn't even catch a cold, but it didn't help my arthritis!

Two nights later, a man and his wife went to visit neighbors across the lake. They both fell into deep water in another part of the lake. She could not swim but he was able to force her up onto the ice. It was pitch dark. Can you imagine their fright?

For the rest of my ice fishing days, I wore a life jacket and carried a long bamboo pole over my shoulders. It may have looked silly but it made me feel a lot safer.

For a lake that my husband said had no damn fish in it, I surely have cleaned and filleted zillions of fish!

Spring brought pussy willows. At the same time, the maple sap began to run. My husband tapped the trees and gathered buckets of sap. These he'd boil off in a large stainless steel vat outdoors. It was a great deal of work, and it brought tremendous satisfaction. We are all addicted to pancakes and maple syrup.

Spring brought all forms of new life. The yards were full of baby geese and ducks and bunnies. Several times, Mike came upon new fawns in our wood lot.

It seemed that every bird in our state, at some time or other, visited or nested around the lake. The first time that we saw the huge pileated woodpeckers tackling a rotting tree, we almost all fell out the window. These birds are at least sixteen inches tall. Their beaks must be four inches long. We once saw five of these fledglings in a tree in our yard.

In summer, we chased insects and butterflies. We made collections of mounted moths, butterflies and beetles for our 4-H Club, which took blue ribbons at the county fair.

Our dock was located in a very good swimming area. It was all a sand bottom. On warm summer days; only food lured the swimmers out of the lake.

Late one August evening, we were returning from the far end of the lake. It was getting dusk and we couldn't tell what was splashing toward shore near the lily pads. We rowed toward the spot as fast as we could. We thought, ducks? dog? snorkelers? When we finally drew near, we had chased the swimmer out into deep water. It was a buck deer with a big rack of velvet horns. He was out cooling off and escaping those pesky deer flies.

I said "watch when he goes on shore; he'll be really pretty!"

We sat disappointed, as he faded into the reeds. Then as we were moping, he jumped over a willow with a full moon as a backdrop. That was one of the neatest animal memories that we had.

Because I had been raised on a trout stream, I taught the boys to trout fish. They eventually both became fanatics. I apologize to their future wives! Trout fishermen are nuts!

Once, Steve came home all excited. He had caught a twelve inch trout with a huge lump in it. We cleaned it and inside was a large furry mouse! That story is only topped by the fact that one time about in the same place, he saw a trout leap out of the water and swallow a mouse that was running on a mossy log.

Another time, Mike was snorkeling when a big Northern came out of the deep misty green and ate an eighteen inch Northern that he was watching.

The neighbor boys all had motor bikes. Our poor children had none! I was about to give in and buy them one.

One day all the boys were gathered out on the road. I had just thought, "Well, at least they're sharing their bikes!"

Mike came running, "Mama, Mama, my brother's hurt bad!"

I ran over and here is Steve in hysterics because they are cutting a new and very bloody shirt off of him.

His cousin offered to let him ride his bike. Coming down the hill at a very fast pace he forgot to brake. He and bike and cousin went through five strands of barbed wire. The cousin fell off and over. Son went through, to the tune of fifty-four stitches.

We thanked God that they were all alive. Our family gave up the idea of motor bikes. Trout fishing was safer.

On the wall at the cottage, we have a sixteen inch brook trout, 18-inch brown trout, and twenty-two inch stream rainbow trout mounted. They're quite impressive, especially to the angler who caught them. Steve caught two and Chet caught one.

My husband and I went out fishing very close to the cottage. It thundered. There was one cloud that covered the sun. It began to rain huge drops. They were warm. They bounced up like ghosts that people make out of napkins at Halloween time. They were at least four inches tall. It was such a beautiful sight. The sound they made couldn't be described. We were warm because the air was warm.

What happened next was surreal. Over in the channel was the brilliant foot of a rainbow that arched across the sky in front of us. It was a double and doubly brilliant set of rainbows. We never found the pot of gold but in that channel was the foot of our very own rainbow. No one else was on the lake. Through the foot of that rainbow, you could see the trees on the opposite shore.

Autumn brought mushrooms, puff balls, and hazel nuts. You ought to try vanilla ice cream with maple syrup and hazel nuts!

TWISTED VINES – An Autobiography of an Ex-Nun

No fish in
this damn
lake! Hey
Dad?

The boys are on skates.

Gorgeous Luna Moth

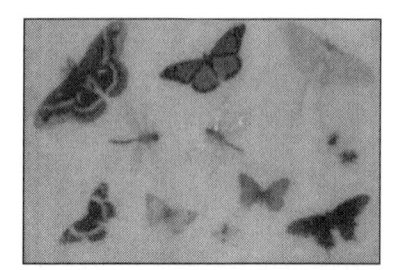

Our insect collection for 4-H.

Steve fell in love with turtles early in life.

Steve's daughter, Lauren.

TWISTED VINES – An Autobiography of an Ex-Nun

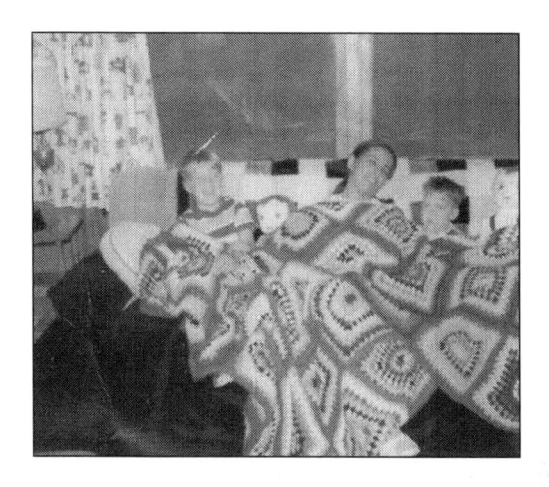

Sister Agnes and her "boys"!

# Fifty-Three

## SNAKES ALIVE!

My mother was an integral part of our life. She was very attached to the boys because they were the youngest of her grandchildren. They were also the only ones who ever grew up near her. They were her pride and joy, also.

When the youngest boy was four, Mom had a stroke. It was a long recovery but she was the winner. She went to a nursing home, one hundred miles away, where my sister was an administrator. It was difficult for us to adjust to her absence but we made the trip at least once a month. Later, she was able to live in a little house there that belonged to my sister, Helen. The boys enjoyed going to visit her.

Many of the boys' fun experiences started at her house. We found two different kinds of turtle eggs that we hatched in our backyard.

We hatched three different kinds of snakes from eggs. That might sound terrible but it was a wonderfully fascinating experience. How many students get to take an egg to Show and Tell, with a tiny snake or turtle peeking out?

One time, we caught a huge fox snake at the river by Grandma's. It was over five feet long. We soaked it in a pail of water to help it shed its skin. One of the boys forgot to cover the container.

A neighbor, a block away, called and told us about the huge snake they found. They had raked it into a garbage can and called the police. They called us because they thought it was someone's exotic tropical snake that had escaped. They knew we'd probably like to see it.

We took our culprit home and told the neighbors to tell the police it got away.

Another day, Steve took his pet out for exercise. It started to crawl near the car. He wanted to know if that was all right and I couldn't think of any reason why it wasn't.

Two minutes later, I knew better. The snake crawled into the shocks of the car. I poked and poked at it. By now, it was agitated and I was afraid of it. It slithered out; and before I could grab it with both hands, it slid into the exhaust system.

Now, my goose was fried! My husband would die of a heart attack if he were driving and that snake decided to be his passenger.

I called a local automotive garage and asked if they would put my car up on their hydraulic hoist so that I could retrieve a snake. "No problem," they said.

The car was up in the air. I worked, and pulled and eventually retracted our five foot plus pine (fox) snake. I looked for the attendant to ask what I owed him. He was sort of cowering over by the gas pumps. "Lady," he said, "I thought you meant a twelve-inch snake! You don't owe us anything! It's not every day that something like this happens!"

We took our snake home and fed him a dead red squirrel. When the cottagers shot red squirrels or chipmunks, we collected and froze them. Once a week, we would thaw one out. When it lay in the sun and became warm, our snake had his weekly repast. Eventually, we let the snake go.

The only reason we had kept it was that we were hoping it would lay eggs. We finally learned that it was a male and it would never fulfill our dreams!

There was another species of snake that provided us much

entertainment. It's the hog nose snake. This is a very ugly, very frightening, perfectly harmless snake! It grows to be only about thirty inches long. It has a funny curled end to its rather short stubby body. Its ugly, ugly, ugly! When this snake is confronted by surprise, it rears up and puffs its head up with a menacing hissing sound. The snake prefers a diet of only toads, but in our area has adapted to frogs. It reminds people of a cobra.

I always caught all the snakes. My boys were supposed to know that they only touched them or played with them after they were calmed down. Most snakes can or will bite if surprised. In our area, no snake that we could likely have caught was dangerous or poisonous. The grown-ups in our vicinity were, without question, positive that the kids and I were nuts. They were also convinced that all snakes should be dead. Snakes did not come after us! We hunted for them! They were not abundant. These stories take place over perhaps 20 years.

One day, when Steve was four years old, he came upon the biggest hog-nosed snake that I have ever seen. He picked it up to bring it to his mother, who would surely be impressed. On the way, he went to show it to relatives who were sitting around a campfire. They all screamed and told him to drop it.

I also must tell you that this snake, in order to frighten my son, up-chucked frogs all along the way, as he was carrying it. That really endeared it to the relatives!

Finally, the lad reached our cottage. He banged on the door. I went to see what he wanted. He was expecting a warm welcome from me. What he got was a screaming maniacal Mother who yelled, "Drop that thing!"

Drop it he did and that snake, just like The World Book Encyclopedia said it would, laid belly up – mouth open, and played dead!

Another time we found a wounded garter snake that a neighbor had tried to kill with a spade. It was paralyzed from about ten inches from its head. Therefore, it could move only with great effort, dragging its stiffened body.

By the swollen abdomen, we knew it was pregnant. This snake has its babies alive. So here was a new science experiment for us.

We bathed and bandaged our captive. We fed her long after it was time for her species to give birth. One day there was a dead rubbery baby snake in the cage.

It was becoming late fall and our snake would never survive winter hibernation. I chloroformed her and we dissected her. She had about an eighteen inch birth canal which contained probably two dozen glistening baby snakes, each in their own placental pouch. They were all dead because she was paralyzed and couldn't give birth.

Once when my boys were little, we came across a red belly snake that was having babies in the warmth of the sand by the creek. We watched with awe as the babies kept coming!

A new neighbor came up from the lake with a cinnamon snake. It looked exhausted and depleted of muscle tone. She said, "Down, at the lake, it was all covered with 'red worms'!" I had someone run down to check. They were all gone. She had had her babies!

One of Michael's first words was "Sneak! Sneak!" as he ran behind a huge fox snake. I certainly followed him to make sure nothing untoward happened to either him or the snake.

Once 5-6 years ago, Chet called me, "Hurry into the garage", I'm thinking, "I'll beat him if he's calling me needlessly." There was a gorgeous newly hatched milk snake slithering sideways across the cement. My mind thought, "Be careful." That's a sidewinder. It was the only way it could move on cement. I think it was attracted to the smell of our woodpile. I went on my scooter, carrying my grabber, recognizing the hatching stage of Fox snakes around Labor Day. I found three more snakes that were not happy about being so ruthlessly scooped up with my grabber. I kept them in a terrarium in the house. They wouldn't eat earthworms. I called the Wildlife Sanctuary who said they were related to the King snakes in California and ate other snakes. I know they used to live around barnyards and eat rodents. When these snakes hatch, there are several other snakes that hatch and are 5-6 inches long. So in the wild, I suspect their evening repasts are baby cinnamon, green grass, or Dekay snakes.

At any rate, I bought baby frozen mice, warmed one up for each of them once a week and they were happy! It was fascinating to watch them unhinge their jaw and work down their meal.

We don't seem to have any snakes around anymore. I definitely blame the milk snakes.

I'd like to see them eat a snake. I've seen them eat 4-5 inch salamanders in a terrarium.

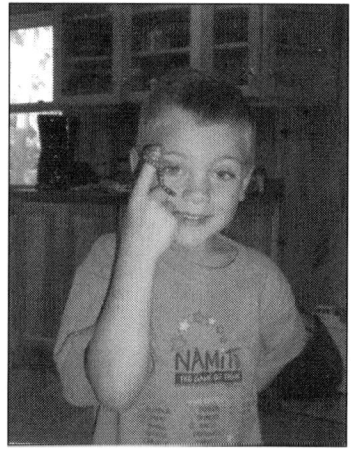

Newly hatched milk snake.

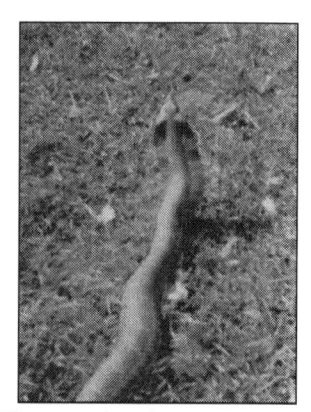

Hog nosed snake or sometimes called puff adder.

I forgot to mention that those baby milk snakes shed their skin twice while I had them. Talk about fascination as we watched them! For a long time I kept those skins displayed above their terrarium.

TWISTED VINES – An Autobiography of an Ex-Nun

*"Our old man of the sea".*
This is my favorite picture of Chet at the cottage.

"No fish, hey, Dad?"

The mighty Eagle.

A painted turtle laying eggs

Mike and Steve with a cinnamon snake.

Huge snapping turtle laying eggs.

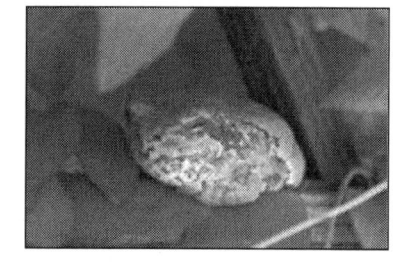

A great singer in Spring. This frog is the grey tree frog.
It turns brilliant green when near leaves.

## Fifty-Four

## NATURE ENTERTAINS US

Many happy hours were spent trying to catch baby painted turtles. We used the wedding veil nets on a long pole. The nets replaced regular fishing nets, as they had too large spaces.

To catch little turtles is not an easy accomplishment. There aren't a lot of them so you really have to search. They are very elusive as they have to avoid heron and bass and other enemies.

It was very difficult to get the boys to understand that you had to net under the turtle. Not on top of them. They always escaped downward.

They were so pretty! The males are real bright orange, red, green and yellow. The females always have a light yellow plastron.

We'd work so hard to catch them and show them off, have races in the sand pit and then let them go.

One turtle had a hole in its shell from a motor boat. We caught it 4-5 years in a row.

Sometimes you'd come upon a little one in a warm puddle of water on top of a lily pad. The smaller the turtle the more joy was involved. We'd actually thank God for the gift and beauty of a turtle!

<u>Loons</u>

Our lake always has a resident pair of loons. We had been

watching a female on her nest with our binoculars.

Once we rowed close to her nest. She was drooped over her nest with her head flat down in the mud. We were all angry because we thought someone had shot her. One of our friends said, "Watch her eyes, they're blinking!" Sure enough, our dead loon was playing possum!

Two days later, Chet and I were fishing in that general area. The male came to the front of our boat calling loon calls, laughing and howling just like a wolf. He actually swam under our boat. Under water he just mesmerized us.

At the nest, we saw the female and two baby chicks slide into the water. The male joined them and they swam along shore with the two babies between them, cooing to them.

Eagles and osprey almost daily gave a show over the lake. Herons ate little fish. Otters just ate and ate and ate!

Mink and muskrat are daily shows on the shoreline.

With all the predators, it's amazing how full of life the lake is. What a wonderful world to observe and study!

Also, one must not miss the marvelous microscopic life in the lake.

Besides which the lake bottom is filled with the nymphs of insects. Life at a lake is truly fantastic!

## Fifty-Five

## OH FOR A SON'S ADULATION

When we were catching butterflies and other insects, we had trouble keeping our nylon netting from rotting in the sun. I got tired of sewing netting. I finally decided to use my wedding veil. Someone had borrowed it and burned a cigarette hole in it, and I was no longer attached to it.

One day I had sewed up a bunch of nets and I said, "Well, that's the end of my wedding veil."

Steve was four. He said, "You're kidding!"

I said, "No, I'll never need it again."

Son says, "You will, too!"

Knowing that he was very serious, I said, "What do you mean?"

He said, "You're going to marry me when I grow up!"

"Oh," I said, "When you want to get married, let me know; I'll sew the nets back together for a veil and we'll get married in the meadow. O.K.?" He was very content.

Another time this same son was watching travel movies. I said, "When you grow up and you go to these different countries, you will take pictures and show me when you come back, won't you?"

He said, "Well, you're coming with me!"

I countered with, "Think about it. When you're big enough to do this by yourself, I'll be too old to keep up!"

This wonderful son of mine said, "I'll walk real slow!"

Such a wonderful son! In a few months the big pup is going to marry a really lovely young lady. They're going to Australia on a honeymoon and at latest report; they do not intend to take me!

When Mike was in third grade, we had some kind of altercation. He called me, "a f-----"and ran off to school. He knew that I could never catch him.

What he didn't expect was that I would take my famous lathe (that I usually just had to look at) and drive to school. Classes had not yet convened. One white-faced lad was very lucky because the nun who taught the class wouldn't let me kill him! He said his bad words a little more quietly and at a farther distance from me at least for a while!

When Steve was in the early grades, he was given a test to see if he could move into a higher group. Sister was perturbed by one of his answers. The selection was to circle the things that cut. There perhaps was a picture of a (scissors, a rose, a vase, a ball, etc.) He had circled, among other things, the vase. I questioned him, "Steve, why did you circle the vase? It wouldn't cut!" "It would too," he retorted, "if you broke it!" Children are amazing.

# Fifty-Six

## MOM RETURNS TO HER GOD

My mother left the nursing home and lived in a lovely little home in Blackwell, Wisconsin that belonged to my sister, Helen Henkel. There she was well and happy and did not pick up all the germs that go around in a nursing home.

Every other week, a priest went to the nursing home to say Mass. He picked Mom up for Mass and they returned to her house. He played her Hammond Organ as she made breakfast for the two of them. She often said she thought of him as a grandson.

Another priest from a different parish had Mass on the opposite weekend. Mom became well acquainted with him. He seemed to have an educational background comparable to my brother in Georgia. This priest was criticized by the parish. He was a recovering alcoholic. He sometimes called my mother late at night and stopped and visited with her when he was afraid he'd be tempted to drink. She said she thought of him as a son.

Mom had surgery and was in the hospital quite a while. Apparently while there, a hospital chaplain spoke to her often in her preparation for death.

Health was on Mom's side and she recuperated. Several weeks later, she got the idea of throwing a party. In her view, it was the

Mother of all parties! Does that sound familiar? Like Mother, like daughter! When she told me about it, I cringed. I wanted to say, "Oh, Mom! Not again!"

She was celebrating her thirty-fifth anniversary of Baptism and her eighty-sixth birthday. She wanted all the relatives to attend Saturday afternoon Mass and then come to dinner at the little town hall just across the street from her home.

My thought was, "here we go again!" Almost all these relatives were non-Catholic and I didn't know how they'd react. She made a few calls and everything was a go!

Two days before the party, Mom didn't answer her phone. I called my sister who said that Mom had fainted the night before and was staying with her. During the call, Mom came to the phone. I said, "Mom, why don't you take it easy Saturday, and just go to dinner, instead of trying to go to church?

She said, "I can't think of a better place to die, than in Church, can you?"

I said goodbye. My sister said that Mom sat down and said, "I'm not going to that party. I'm sick! Call a priest."

My sister said, "Well, if you're sick, don't you think a doctor would be better than a priest?"

"No," Mom said, "Call a priest."

My sister did. Then she called an ambulance. The priest, who was like her own son, came and administered to Mom. He said later that he never dreamed that anything was seriously wrong with her.

At three p.m., my sister called. She said, "I'm sure I goofed up that party for tomorrow. Mom threw her new house robe at me and told me to take it home. She wouldn't need it."

We got to the cottage at 5:00 p.m. The neighbor came running out to say there was a message that Mom was critical and I should leave immediately.

It was a one hundred-fifty mile trip in extremely dense fog. I stopped at my sister's and unloaded all my party food.

When I got to the hospital, the doctor explained that he had not been able to insert a pacemaker and Mom wanted him to quit trying. She was tired. He said she wouldn't gain consciousness or recognize me, but if I wanted to see her alive, to go in quickly. My sister and her husband also went in.

Mom looked up as I came in. She said, "What time is it?" Then she shook her head to think that I was out so late. She looked out and saw how foggy it was. She said, "How are Chet and the boys?"

A priest came in dressed in lay clothing. It was now midnight. Mom greeted him and thanked him for helping her die. His eyes filled with tears and he said, "That's a first. No one has ever thanked me before for helping them die."

Soon after, the monitor went blank. The doctor called my brother and told him Mom had died.

My sister said, "Can she be dead and still have a pulse?"

Doctor said, "That's just nerves."

Well, Mom gulped and said, "I'm still here!" (One of us had accidentally kicked the monitor cord!)

Doctor went out and retracted the information he had relayed to my brother.

Priest said, 'Did you hear anything while you were gone, Maude?"

Mom said, "No."

Priest said, "Did you see Jesus while you were gone?"

Mom said, "I don't think I'd recognize Him if I saw Him." Everybody gasped!

Priest said, "You know, that's an honest answer. People who lived with Him didn't recognize Him. He's in everyone we meet today and we don't recognize Him."

Mom said, "I'm glad I'm in the hospital."

"Why, Mom, do you hurt?" I asked.

She wiggled her toes. "No," she said, "I don't hurt anywhere."

Doctor said, "She's too far gone to hurt."

"Then, Mom, why are you glad you're in the hospital?" I asked.

"So that no one has to baby sit me during the party," was her answer.

"Mom," I said, "Will you forget that party?"

She almost sat up. "You <u>promise</u> me that you will all go to Church and that you'll have a party!"

"Yes, Ma!"

"I'm ready to die now," she announced.

I watched very carefully. She pushed like she was giving birth and she was gone.

Later, I mentioned to the doctor that this was the first death I had ever seen.

He said, "Death is not usually like this. This lady went out in style!"

It was 2:00 a.m. Mom's party was to begin at 4:00 p.m. that evening at church.

The priest came up the aisle and started to cry. He went to the podium and said, "I just remembered that this was the song Maude always played for me when I visited her. It's been a very rough week on me. My brother's home burned down earlier this week and he lost all his possessions. Maude's possessions were the kind that nobody could take from her. I lost a very good friend when she died."

This priest was thirty-seven years old and there was that kind of a bond, between him, and my mother, who was eighty-six.

We had Mom's Party. We all attended Mass and went to the town hall. We cried and laughed and ate and started all over again! I know that she was there.

We arranged for the funeral. The grandchildren were all to be pallbearers. They were all grown men. Everyone seemed to forget that my children, nine and twelve, were grandchildren. They had enough pallbearers and I was willing to let them be forgotten.

My youngest son, Mike, wasn't about to forget. He made a big pain of himself, interrupting the grownups who were sadly making decisions. The mortician asked me what the problem was. I explained and told him how our oldest son couldn't do it anyway, because he'd just had surgery and couldn't lift anything. The mortician said that was no problem. There could be any number of pallbearers and my sons didn't have to lift.

Then this wonderful man turned to my persistent son and said, "Young man, for the rest of your life, remember if you really want something - go for it!"

That's how the casket never moved an inch without Mom's youngest grandsons helping.

The funeral cortege was led by the priest who was a recovering alcoholic. We drove for fifty miles on roads that wound through hardwood forests. The woodland surfaces were covered with trilliums and other wild flowers.

. At the funeral service, the priest turned to us and said, "You will never know what a supporter of the priesthood your Mother was. She was praying for priest vocations in her own family."

My mother and Rae Lynn, a great granddaughter.

The dragonfly metamorphosis.

This is just the empty case – like an empty chrysalis.

# Fifty-Seven

## TEMPORARY EMPLOYMENT

For years, I had worked for Temporary Employment Services in Green Bay doing around the clock shiftwork at factories and mills. One reason was to get a better feeling of what life was like for the blue collar worker. The over-riding reason was to get my sons out of dependency on my sphere of influence. It forced them to grow up and me to let them. I could see that they were growing away from me and I had better fill my life with something else or it would become lonely and painful, indeed when they left.

Several places where I worked showed respect for their temporary workers. Most by far, did not! They hired people at a much lower salary than their regular workers. They often worked longer hours and with no benefits.

Some places didn't even demonstrate or train the worker. They were just shown where to go.

Several times a new worker would come in and ask for "Pat" to explain what she should do. There were two Pat's and the full time worker, actually in charge, ignored the newcomer. I ignored her because I had no clout in the job. It wasn't my responsibility.

I told the head of the Employment Service what had happened. She said she had actually sent her to me because the situation was so bad at that factory. No one wanted part-time employment workers, as they saw it as threatening their jobs. Therefore they treated them like scabs.

At the cheese factory, I was told to clean out a group of machines. It was a food establishment and the machines were filthy. I finished and the owner said I could go home.

"I have to work four hours, sir, in order to be paid."

Then go clean out the cans (toilets) he said.

I finished and asked what else I should do.

"Go work on that line!" was his answer.

"Sir, I can't go work on your food line. You just had me cleaning out toilets!"

That was the last time I worked at that cheese factory.

On the flip side, I saw workers steal tape and equipment left laying around. They put them in their coats as they left. One woman stole four sets of very expensive drill bits. She somehow put them in her slacks or bra!

At an ice cream factory they had trouble with flies. A woman who was in an enclosed plastic work area, receiving chocolate chip ice cream, used to break up flies and put them in the ice cream. She thought that was hilarious.

There was absolutely no respect given to these part-time workers. Production was the only thing that counted. There were no rewards for achievement therefore some workers took every advantage that they could from the employer.

I was shocked to hear that a woman I knew at the ice cream factory died of a heart attack while working on the line. Someone took her place and production kept right on.

The woman had worked at this place for many years. It was too expensive to stop and re-start that machine. So work kept right on for her co-workers! I still find this hard to fathom.

# Fifty-Eight

## LADY SLIPPERS

Once I was working at a job with a relative. Our job ended and there was no immediate employment. She convinced me to answer housecleaning ads. Soon she found a full-time job and I was cleaning houses five days a week. I did that for about five years.

One day while cleaning a window, it was hard not to notice that a girl and her boyfriend were having sex in the parlor. Her mother eventually went in and asked her to pick up a half-dozen pair of shoes.

I figured as long as the mother wasn't disturbed, I surely must have been seeing things. I went back to "re-clean" the window and check on my grasp of reality. There was no question that they were engaged in mad, passionate sex, only this time in a different position!

I had begun to go to a counselor for weight loss. I now stormed into his office and said, "Either I'm nuts or the world's nuts and you are about to help me sort it out!"

I spent over a hundred hours over a two-year period with that counselor. I paid fifty-five dollars an hour, which I earned by cleaning other people's houses. Someone had to walk through my soul with me and help me figure life out. We wrestled every aspect of life, much like a dog chewing on a bone. Eventually, the fog in my life and brain settled. After much expense and pain in the past, today my life is at peace.

I mentioned earlier that when I left the Convent, I had shoved many unsolved issues behind the doors of my unconscious, and locked them tight. One can do that just so long and the steam comes seeping out under the door and through the cracks! At this time, I opened those closet doors and like "Fibber McGee's closet," it all poured out into the open.

The issue of weight was certainly the most noticeable and perhaps the easiest to face. It wasn't the easiest to solve by far. That, I know, is a lifetime battle.

First of all, over-eating is a disorder, an addiction. One cannot give it up, like you perhaps can, alcohol, smoking, or gambling. Food, like air, is a necessity for life. Also, for me, it had been a conscious switch to replace pain killers.

Emotional pain has left, but I am constantly barraged by the physical pain and fatigue of arthritis. I still eat to gain comforting relief which in turn adds weight, which in turn makes my arthritis' pain worse, which in turn, invites me to eat! You see, I like circles! Well, anyway, I'm still working on it.

Behind this eating and weight gain, there is, a subversive force defying my husband and family to love me as I am. Now, they've proven way beyond doubt that they do! Dumb as I am, even I can see that. All that is left and necessary is for my body/mind combination to quit the game! That's much easier said than done. If someone could figure out that key, we Americans would all be thin!

Our family has always been intrigued by nature. We love wild flowers. The height of our searches has always been the North American Orchids, or Lady Slippers. They come in a number of varieties and are located in different terrains.

Forty-five years ago, my sister had transplanted a Showy Lady Slipper from another sister's property in northern Michigan. In May, when it blossomed, it was the center of everyone's interest. The rounded instep of the moccasin is bright rose with deeper stripes. The rest is a translucent white. I always think that it must be reflective of the light of Christ's Resurrection. I know of no other white that is quite like it. The ties are tan-colored.

When my sister was terminally ill, I really wanted to ask her for that flower, but I was sure that her daughter would want it. Later, as we were writing out funeral thank-you notes, her daughter said to me, "Why don't you take Mom's Lady Slipper? Dad will forget and mow it down and I already have one." So now, this flower with its many blossoms thrives under a large tamarack tree on the lakeshore in front of our cottage. Altogether, it has over twenty-five blossoms. The plant stands up over two feet tall.

One of the mental exercises I was to do with my counselor involved imagining many concentric circles within each other. On each one, I was to write a quality representing myself. For example, wife, mother, cook, artist, homemaker, seamstress, etc., etc. In the very center of all of these, there was to appear a picture of something that would represent the core of my existence.

To my surprise, as I was drowning in buckets of tears, my central core was a Lady Slipper. When the counselor asked me the reason for my tears, I explained that I was like the Lady Slipper, delicate and fragile, endangered and hidden where no one ever saw it and knew it existed.

My counselor had been on a canoe trip, with a group, at Ely, Minnesota. He exploded, 'But people really <u>search</u> for Lady Slippers! And when they find them, they kneel in awe!" Point taken!

In one session, I was to go back to my birth. It involved a beautiful journey of imaginings. I came to my mother, giving birth. My arms were holding a bunch of blankets. I was told to give my infant all the love that I knew she needed and somehow didn't get. Once more, I was in tears. I was just holding an armful of empty blankets. There was no child. My very conscious awareness was that I had rejected myself from the very beginning, in order to avoid the pain of rejection from others! I had practically rejected my own existence. So that was from where my problem began! I was imbued with the thought, "How could I be so damn dumb?"

Several weeks later, I got brave enough to attempt the exercise again. This time before finding the woman giving birth, I was to rest under a tree where a messenger would come to me. Immediately, I envisioned a magnificent warrior angel striding over the hill. He bent on one knee before me, holding a vessel or pot of molten gold. All he said was, "Look, this has been your life."

My search was ended. I was completely at rest on the issue of the worth and value of my life. I could add no more love to my existence than I had already been given. All I needed to do was to recognize and accept it as what had always been mine.

One time, in a group session devoted to healing work, we again followed a guided meditation. This was led by a priest. Once again, the leader said, "A messenger will come to you with a gift."

One person's messenger was a butterfly; another one, a lion, etc. When I went around the corner, there sat a very modest angel dressed in a simple, white robe. He looked me straight in the eye, and held up a gold cross for me to take.

By now, I was tired of crosses. I would have liked to have been given another gift. I really struggled with this. My counselor encouraged me to accept it. So, I took it, halfway resignedly and half-willingly. I hope to carry it more joyfully than in the past, until such time as I can lay it down and join Christ in His Resurrected Glory.

When I first went to counseling, I said, "If I could tell you that my husband or children were a part of my problems, it would make more sense, but they're just not."

To which, he replied, "You're very lucky. You can't change others. The only one you can change is yourself." This counselor seldom spoke. Either he listened to me wrangle with my own struggles, or we worked with hypnosis, during our hours together. When he did speak, his words were succinct and to the point, and they carried meaning for me that I will never forget.

One day, I was in a great deal of turmoil. I stepped into a church to visit the Blessed Sacrament. It was like I heard a voice telling me to look up a certain priest. As far as I knew, he should have been on a mission in Wyoming. I called and sure enough, he was available in the locality.

When I had known this priest, thirty years before, I had thought of him as a dominant prepossessive person. As I entered the foyer of the building in which I was to meet him, I saw a poor, feeble man whom I thought was a man off the street who had come to the monastery for help. Only a flicker of recognition in his eye told me that this was the priest whom I had asked to "warm" me back to Christ. Warm me back, he did! I didn't know that priests could be so human!

As I left that day, he invited me to make a retreat that he was helping give five months from then. I maintained, "No," – I couldn't do that. I had a husband and family, job and dog, to take care of. This wonderful priest had one word to say – and he said it, forcefully, "Bull Crap!"

"Well," I said, "You can say whatever you want, Father, but it can't be done!"

So I went back to my struggles.

My favorite lady slippers.

## Fifty-Nine

## SUPER MARIO BROTHERS

Christmas came. I made one big effort to shop in the Malls. I knew that the boys wanted the electronic Nintendo. In one shop, the salesman said, "We only have five of these left. They contain the game <u>Super Mario Brothers</u>. It's almost impossible to purchase these anywhere, anymore.

I wasn't interested in a sales pitch. I really didn't have the least bit of interest in Nintendo. I knew nothing about it, and didn't intend to learn, so I didn't listen to him.

I sat outside the store on a bench and mulled it over, along with my financial status. Finally, I decided if that's what the kids wanted, I'd buy it and get it over with. I had it gift-wrapped and took it home.

Three weeks later, I said to the boys, "Say, I was to buy a Nintendo set. If I was so disposed as to buy an extra game, which one would you like?"

Oh! No question! They wanted one called Super Mario Brothers! So off I went in an unattainable quest. It was now a week before Christmas. Sales people just laughed at me. It simply couldn't be purchased.

Well, by golly, I was going to get that game! I called every store in our city – all to no avail. I called a niece in California, a brother in Georgia. A friend was a buyer for a special gift store. She checked Chicago and New York. No way – couldn't be had!

One day, I called a store thinking maybe a new shipment came in. "Oh, yes," said the saleslady, "we have two, but I can't hold them."

I dashed out the door. Five minutes later, I approached her counter to see her hand <u>my</u> game to another lady with a sales slip. I heard her say, "I hope that was the lady who just called me!"

On my way to work that day, I was lucky no one was on the highway behind me. A thought struck my brain and I slammed on my brakes. Not a smart thing to do, but by now, you know that I'm not renowned for my brilliance.

In a beautifully wrapped package, under my decorated Christmas tree, was a Nintendo set with <u>Mario Brothers</u> in it!

There were two extremely happy boys that Christmas morning! Our basement had a wide assortment of "friends" for several weeks. Their moms hadn't been able to find <u>Super Mario Brothers</u>."

I told my counselor about my search and discovery. He said, "That's almost always the case. Our happiness is right under our own nose. We just don't look in the right place."

It's kind of like the phrase, "Blossom where you grow." If a daisy on the hillside refused to bloom and said, "I wish I were a rose on the opposite ridge," we'd never see the exquisite beauty of the gold and brown of the brown-eyed Susan or the white and gold, if it were of an ox-eye daisy.

I once said to my counselor, "If my husband or sons could hear what I was saying, or see me cringe and hide my face when I expressed an opinion that I felt strongly about, they would never have recognized me. It was the child within that needed to hide and cringe, and it's taken more than ten years for that child to learn to talk and play freely!"

I think that our subconscious may someday be discovered as much more important than our conscious cognitive faculties. If one wants to learn new material, they are to study that material, uninterrupted, before sleep. Once the studying is done, if one sleeps, very often the material has been assimilated by the brain, when one wakens.

Many important issues of my life have been solved during sleep. I knew that we should not ignore our sub-conscious. I have made a lifetime habit of stuffing unsolved issues and pain beneath the level of my conscious surface. It's so habitual that even now when I try very hard not to do that, it still happens.

Then I find myself thinking, "Why do I feel badly? What on earth did I just stuff?"

Usually, with enough ferreting, especially if it was just buried, I can dig the little bugger out of its hold and handle it. I know from a lifetime of experience that, like an iceberg, the conscious is like the part that is visible. The largest part of the weighty mass is below the surface.

While I was in counseling, I had a powerful dream. I was sleeping and someone came and told me that my child was dying, and I was to go to him. I ran, expecting to find one of my children. There, along the roadway, in the dark, was a large buck deer. I bent down to help it and it got up and began to gore me.

It said, "I am your child within, and if you do not take care of me now, I will kill you. You have ignored me for the last time!"

The message was well-received and I now consciously try to take care of the little child within me. I certainly had ignored her too long. She had every right to rebel!

# *Sixty*

## RETREATS

*A*bout that time, I picked up the phone and said to my old priest friend, "Where and when did you say you were helping give a retreat?"

I knew very well that it was the next day and about seventy miles away. Lo and behold, husband, kids, and dog all supported me! Weren't those big obstacles? As Father said, "My excuses were bull crap!"

Two things really hit me. One was being wrapped up in a tight circle of people and occurred one night, during reunion. Later, we all went around an altar and my tears flooded the sanctuary. I know people expected me to open up, but tears came, not words. Words came later, and now in writing!

This retreat took place at the height of my struggle with weight. On the first night, we were all given a Bible. Inside the cover was a different Bible quotation for each candidate. These were passed out at random.

My verse was Matthew, Chapter 4, verse 4. It says, "Then the Spirit led Jesus into the desert to be tempted by the Devil. After spending forty days and nights without food, Jesus was hungry. Then the Devil came to Him and said, "If you are the Son of God, order these stones to turn into bread."

But Jesus answered, "The scripture says, "Man cannot live on bread alone, but needs every word that God speaks."

For a long time, I concentrated on the bread and worried about my food addiction.

A year later, I had the privilege of making a Fifteen Week Retreat. It was an adaptation of St. Ignatius' Thirty Day Retreat for priests.

It was rewritten by a Franciscan priest for lay men and women. It involved fifteen minutes of directed Scripture reading a day, followed by fifteen minutes of absolute silence, during which we were to listen to the Holy Spirit speak to our hearts. Then we were to write our thoughts, aspirations, and prayers in a notebook. We did this for fifteen weeks. It was highly recommended that we curtail T.V. and extra-curricular reading for this period. We met once a week and shared our thoughts. We were to be guided but not criticized.

For me, it was marvelous. I often spent far more time on Scripture than required. At the time, I had two or three hours home alone every day before I went to work.

When the retreat was finished, I wished that it could have gone on forever. The priest who had invited me to the original retreat decided to be a candidate for this fifteen week episode.

I gave him a ride to and from the retreat location, in which we had an hour to confer together weekly. It was wonderful for me to witness this priest as a fellow traveler on the journey of life and the quest of the soul. I was amazed at the humility of both the priest who was a leader and my friend who was a fellow-retreatant. We had about six other co-candidates. I was amazed at everyone's candor and trust. I was humbled by some things and absolutely astonished by others. I remember searching the priests' faces during some of the things people said. I thought, "Are you going to let them get away with that?"

Actually, I was being introduced to the lay Catholics and I was finding them to be wonderful creatures!

Somehow with my own home and convent background, I found it

very hard to adapt to parish life. I just, once more, didn't seem to fit in. This experience and my years later of helping direct these retreats, gave me a spiritual home into which I fit.

Once the retreat ended, I discovered that I had acquired at least one wonderful habit in my life – the study of Holy Scripture. That has become a life-long avocation.

It took a long time for me to realize how deeply the Old and New Testaments are related. To check out those references on the bottom of the pages is a real education.

For instance, my reading in Matt. 4:4 has a tremendous counterpart in Deuteronomy 8:3. It still sends shivers down my spine. It says, "He made you go hungry, and then gave you Manna to eat, food that you and your ancestors had never eaten before. He did this to teach you that man must not depend on bread alone to sustain him, but on everything that the Lord says."

I was still attending group sessions for weight loss. I never lost a lot of weight but I sure shed a lot of heavy baggage. I also made some very good friends. One week, we were supposed to write down all the sub-conscious wishes that you heard yourself desiring during the week. I had quite a list!

## Sixty-One

## ARE YOU HIRING PEOPLE?

One morning I simply didn't feel like cleaning anyone's house. I was to clean the halls and recreation areas of a large complex of apartments that day. It wasn't necessary to do it that exact day so I begged off until later in the week.

The next day was my husband's birthday. I went on the other side of town to locate a large men's clothing store. It had moved locations. However, on that block was a brand-new, very large grocery store. I thought that I might as well check it out, in I went.

I had never been in a store for a grand opening. The multitudinous check-out lines went all the way to the back of the store. I wandered through like a kid in a candy store. There was music and color, and everywhere I went, I heard cheerful voices saying to people, "May I help you? May I help you?"

I remember laughing and going out of the store without purchasing anything. I felt like a clown doing somersaults, all the way home. My thought was, "I sure would like to work in a place like that!"

I sat at the table and jotted down my sub-conscious wish. Then I picked up the phone, dialed Copp's Food Store, "Are you hiring people?"

The lady said, "Up to now, we had to hire from Job Service. Now that we're open, I could hire. Did you fill out an application?"

"No," I said, "I just now thought about it."

She said, "Why don't you come and fill out an application?"

Now, I really wasn't looking for a job but out of my mouth popped, "If I do, can I have an interview?"

One was granted for an hour later. I never did get the interview. The lady said, "I didn't know what I wanted you for, but when I set the phone down, the manager said, "We need a demo lady." And she answered, "I have one." The next day, I handed out twelve hundred and fifty nine samples and spoke directly to each of those people.

My one regret about having left the Convent was being out of the flow of people. That problem was solved.

14 years later, I was still working in the same capacity for a company that I really love. I am surrounded every day by loving people. This to me is pure gift from God. I also try to return this back as pure gift to God. At times at least, I've made a great effort to treat each person who comes to my table as I would treat Christ.

Sometimes this becomes quite a struggle. I've read that when we don't like someone, it's because we see something in ourself that is like that person. I do know that often when I have met someone whom I really didn't like, upon better acquaintance, we have become good friends.

One day, soon after I started my new job as food demonstrator, I entered the meat department to see a crowd of people scrambling and searching through a bunker. It was a "buy one, get one" free deal. The scene that came to my mind was a bunch of carrion beetles fighting and clawing over road kill. Greed was plainly printed on the people's faces. The thought that struck me like a bolt of lightning was, "And God became <u>one</u> of <u>us</u>? Not only that, but He <u>died</u> for us to let us go to Heaven? He died for us greedy, clutching people?

One day a man whom I and everyone who knew him have labeled as greedy and miserly, came through the store. Everyone knew that he was more than "filthy rich." I had great difficulty seeing Christ in this man. I forced myself to greet him and be nice. He showed me a cherry pie that was marked down from $3.99 to 99 cents. I followed the flow and said, "You got a <u>cherry</u> pie for that?"

"Sure," he says. "There are two more there. Would you like me to get you one?" He shuffled back and brought me a pie.

Now, I'm a scratch baker. I knew that pie, in my mind, was nothing! But the greed in me had to have that pie! The Christ in the man made him walk with great difficulty in order to get me that pie.

I didn't want a customer to take <u>my</u> pie so I wrapped it with a couple of napkins. It was on my table as I started to leave to wash my pans. It was now closing time.

Up shuffled another old unkempt man. There was no food at my table but his greed made him uncover my pie to see what might have been there. His voice got real high and he squeaked, "This cherry pie is only 99 cents?" And off he scurried with <u>my</u> pie! Laughter bubbled within me. Somehow it was extremely apparent to me that Christ was laughing at me through both of these men.

Often, if I'm forgetful of my mission, some dirty little child that I've been trying to ignore will look at me with soulful eyes and say, "I love you!" I'm jolted by the fact that Christ is speaking to me and I've been tiredly trying to ignore Him.

One day I entered the store and a lady came over and hugged me.

A fellow demonstrator said to me, "Who was that? How do you do that?" I said, "How do I do what?" "I don't know she's just a customer."

She said. "Well I draw a line and the customer has to stay on the other side!" My answer to her was, "I draw a line also, and then I invite them to cross it!"

Men used to visit at my stand as their wives shopped. One time I was telling them about my son, Mike, cooking beaver tail soup. I had just said, "It was delicious!"

A very attractive woman, dressed in high heels and furs went by. She turned and I thought, "Oh boy, I'm in trouble. She probably is from PETA.

"If you like beaver," you should try muskrat!"

She had been raised eating muskrat in South Carolina.

Then the men started opening up. One of them said, "We ate marsh bunnies during WWII, when I was a kid!" It was the only meat we could afford!"

One day I had a sign on my table "Hot appliances."

A man about 22 came and said, "Where's the applesauce?"

"Pardon me," I said. "I don't understand what you mean." He pointed to my sign and said, "It says right there, hot applesauce!"

Each year Copp's had a "summer in winter" contest. I won it four years in a row. One year I dressed as a woman snowman. I was getting ready to demonstrate, and a little girl kept buzzing around. I was still embarrassed as to how I was dressed. She wouldn't leave me alone.

"Hi, Crystal," she said.

"Hi, honey." I answered.

"You don't know who Crystal is, do you?" she exclaimed.

"No, honey, I don't."

"She's Frosty's girlfriend," she replied as she was literally hopping up and down. The rest of the year my manager wrote my name on the work schedule as "Crystal Dudkiewicz".

A young man came up while I was frying *No Name Steak* in a little butter. "How come this doesn't taste like this when I make it?"

"How do you make it?" I asked.

"I boil it", he said.

Sometimes an old person, that society tends to ignore, will put a hand on my shoulder and tell me how much I mean to her or him. The worth of the mission Christ has entrusted to me hits home when something like that happens, and I look up and don't remember having seen the person before. Those people are one on one with me. I'm one on thousands with them and my memory can't contain it all. Actually, I guess all my memory needs to contain is Christ. I am convinced that on my deathbed, I will be very aware that He is all that Is or ever Was.

"Crystal" Dudkiewicz
I worked an 8 hour shift dressed like this!

## Sixty-Two

## THE OTHER SIDE OF THIS DRY DESERT

My sessions in counseling helped me find God. I really ended up in a retreat as a result of my struggles during this time. I also wandered into my wonderful job as a result of soul searching. One time I was worrying the bone called, "Why didn't I find God in the convent?" The counselor said, "Because you were looking for Him up there! He is not so easily found on the vertical line. He is horizontal. You find Him among his people!" Well, that's not what he really said, "It's good enough for me that that's what I <u>heard</u>. At any rate, God has since been much more accessible to me.

There was one more mental exercise that I did in counseling that was very important to me. I seemed always to have this big wall that kept me from a lot of achievement. It was insurmountable.

I was to imagine a wall. It was impenetrable. There was no way to pass through it. So I was told to scale it by using a rope that hung down to its side. I did this. At the top, I comfortably sat and scanned both sides from my resting position. The side I had come from was hot, dry, arid desert covered with thorny cactus. The other side was green, wooded with streams and animals. It was covered with warm, glowing lights in the mist.

I made my decision to get to the other side of the wall. There was no way down on that side, so I this time slid down the rope. Once down, I saw that there was indeed a narrow hidden opening that I could slide through. Beneath the towering wall was a large, moist, moss-covered crypt.

I was told that, hidden in the moss, were signs meant just for me. I saw three. One said, "Trust." One said, "Love," and the other said, "Welcome."

I was to go back and put the signs into my knapsack so that I wouldn't forget the messages when I went to the other side. Also, in my eagerness, I had missed gifts that were there just for me.

I approached the sign, "Trust," and an ice cube floated toward me. I said, "Oh, this isn't a gift. I'm cold and I have to go to the bathroom."

The counselor said, "That may be very true but be real careful. Don't lightly pass up a gift."

I knew even before he was finished speaking that my ice cube was indeed a gift. It was the cold isolation that I would no longer feel, if I went forward into the rest of my life being open and <u>trusting</u>.

The second gift of love was a pink marble heart. It was hollow and opened. It was full of all my past memories. For all my whining and complaining, my memories were all essentially good memories.

The third gift was a round spot or area of warm sunshine. It was God's love for me – my welcome sign to take into the rest of my life.

I stepped through the door into fresh, allergy-free air. All of nature called to me. I was aware, that all the lights glowing through the misty surroundings were the warmth of the love all my fellow beings were offering to me, in my new-found openness.

In a final group work session on weight control, I was sitting in the sun on the beach on a warm rock when an older, slender woman came walking toward me. I recognized her as myself, as she said, "Everything's going to be O.K.!" I stayed behind, alone for a long time, in tears. As I left, the counselor asked me what had happened. I told him and he said, "Trust that! The sub-conscious never lies!" Isn't that wonderful?

# Sixty-Three

## THE PAIN IN OUR LIFE

People who have shared some of this book's early draft have commented on the pain it revealed. My pain has been very, very minor compared to the pain most of the world has experienced. But it has been enough to make me study the subject.

Pain is a question that philosophers from the beginning of time have tossed around and tried to understand. In heaven, we will understand its value. Surely, it is a furnace that purifies gold. In the heating process of pain, the slag of our own sinfulness rises to the top and spews over the vast vat of our souls. If we do not face and embrace the pain in our life, our piece of the mosaic loses its inner beauty.

Our God became one of us and embraced pain from the moment of His birth to His final breath when He said, "It is finished."

What greater pain could be imagined than that expressed by Jesus Christ, God made Man? In Matthew 26: 37-40, it says "Grief and anguish came over Him, and He said to them, 'The sorrow in my heart is so great that it almost crushes me. Stay here and keep watch with Me.'"

He went a little farther on, threw Himself face downward on the ground, and prayed, "My Father, if it is possible, take this cup of suffering from me! Yet not what I want, but what you want."

All of Christ's humanity gathered itself together on the cross to shout in agony, "My God, my God, why have you abandoned Me?"

Whatever our pain, Jesus has gone before, suffered and given us example. He didn't <u>tell</u> us how to deal with it from a throne on high. He came down to our level, became one of us, and showed us. The cross and life seem to go hand in hand. Jesus said, "Follow Me."

Christ's cross, embraced, led him to defeat in the world's eyes.

Our crosses lead us to defeat in the world's eyes. In the light of faith, our Heavenly Father, through the Holy Spirit, leads us with Christ to Eternal life. Through death to self, if we embrace our particular cross, we, too, will share Christ's Eternal life.

Throughout Christ's life, Mary, His Mother, was His support. In the Gospel of John 19: 26-27, Jesus gave His Mother to us when He said, "Jesus saw His mother and the disciple He loved standing there; so He said to His mother, 'He is your son.'"

And then He said to the disciple, "She is your Mother." There are many interpretations to these passages. Whatever they may be, they do not negate Mary's care for us and the fact that she is always there to help us on the journey she and her Son also took.

# Sixty-Four

## PAIN, PAIN, PAIN

I'd like to quit writing but I know that this book, although a cathartic to me, was meant to be of help to others. Therefore, I feel bound to consciously connect these pages into a coherent story.

Over the years, I've had a lot of illness and many surgeries. When I look back, I've never for a moment allowed anyone to think that I was "sickly." I wonder what I would call it??

Actually, I feel like the figure skaters in competition. Each setback is a fall on my butt, but like them, I bounce back and pretend that nothing happened. Sometimes, if you act vigorously enough, one can even convince yourself that nothing has happened!

Years ago, when I had surgery, the doctor said that I had ten hernias in scar tissue, left from previous surgeries, through which my intestines were playing hide and go seek! He sewed up the scar tissues and lashed them to my abdominal wall with nylon mesh. The morning that I was to go home I woke up sobbing, cold, and shaking. They had taken me off morphine and I was going through withdrawal. The nurses were amazed at my emotional upheaval because I had sanguinely weathered the earlier pain of surgery.

I knew by now that this was a medical reaction, because it had happened to me after previous surgeries. I demanded to see the hospital chaplain. "Now?" said the nurse. It was 6:00 A.M.

"Yes," I sobbed, "I can't think of a better time, can you? Now's when I need him!"

The priest came in. I definitely flew in to ruffle his calm demeanor. "Father, do you believe in God?"

"Well, ah, oh, yes!" Then he started giving me his theological hypotheses.

"Oh, Father, cut the crap! I don't give a damn about, etc., etc. I want to know if, in your gut, you really think that there is a God!"

By the time he left, we were both a bit shaken. We'd shared a bit about religious training and seminary or convent formation and we both had a fresh new glimpse of this God issue.

Doctor came in. He was real pleased with his artwork! I left the hospital on some real powerful pain killers. I didn't know that. I just knew that I felt better than I had in twenty years. Doctor said I could do anything that I felt like doing, just not to lift or do stairs. I didn't.

But apparently, I did something that wasn't in the books. I felt so good! I didn't need to rest.

We went to the cottage. I walked around a great deal. I stayed up late by the campfire. The next day I went to Mass. Then we grocery shopped. I knew that leaning over the grocery cart wasn't my best move.

We got home and I made breakfast. Pancakes and maple syrup are always in order Sunday morning at the cottage.

I noticed that my black slacks were all wet in front. I went to the bedroom to check and to my horror, watched that entire ten-inch incision open up, like a Ziploc bag! Now, I'm heavy. That incision was three inches deep.

Remember, I came from a farm originally, where you doctored yourself unless you were dying. I taped it together and took it easy for a couple days. When we returned home and got near the clinic, I got hysterical. "Turn into that clinic," I demanded.

Well, needless to say, no one was real happy with me.

I spent the summer trying to heal and doing every word the

doctor said.

After three months, the incision had to be re-opened because there was an infection at the bottom that wouldn't heal.

So back I went, for more surgery. This time there was no pain but there was a huge gaping hole, left open to heal from the bottom. This was the scariest, awfullest experience of my whole life. There in the middle of my belly was a cauterized, burned hole five inches long, three inches wide, and four inches deep. It looked just like the inside of a silo. Empty silos can kill. This hole killed my spirit.

Once more, I called my old priest friend who came and held me while I sobbed. What a warm human being! And once more he reassured me, "None of us have the answers. We're all struggling along on the same journey!" Somehow that, to me, was much more reassuring than if he'd had all the answers!

I was supposed to have the visiting nurses come and irrigate and pack my wound. I talked them into showing me how to do it each day in the hospital. Like father, like daughter, I guess.

Several days later, I went back to work. When my manager asked, "How come you healed so fast this time?"

I said, "I haven't."

He said, "That's what I thought."

If he had known what I knew, he'd have killed me! It took six months to heal. The doctor said that it could have taken anywhere from two to four years.

At present, I am back to work again, following my Cortisone Party! I would like to spend another ten or fifteen years at this job. Only God knows the future. I trust in Him. My health problems are so many that I am agonizingly conscious of the pending possibilities. Hopefully, God wants me to take care of His people for a long time. "Here I Am, Lord."

# Sixty-Five

## CHANGE IS INEVITABLE

Recently, there was a change in the structure of my job where I work. I no longer had my permanent table. My knives, my pens, pans, etc. were no longer where I could reach in blindly and get what I needed. Truly blind, I could have handled my original table.

I wasn't blind – who knows? I could be some day. But I was "crippled." Don't get excited. I know that handicapped is a better word. But I really was crippled. Just these little things irritated me beyond belief.

Now this is a joke, yet my manager and I both knew, that deep down I wasn't joking, the day I called her on the intercom and said, "Where the hell is my frying pan?"

There was just a little change facing me and I was rebelling. Another manager loves to say, "You're young. You'll adjust," when we're cornered by change.

The older I get the less I like change. I am and always have been a free flowing spirit. My flow had become boxed in, so that instead of a brook gurgling over a clear sand bed, I've been muddy, agitated water going around and around locked in a dark cylindrical washer.

If I mind change, think how hard it is for statistical minds, whose lives depend on things fitting into neat squares and balancing out to the penny.

Life changes. We have only today. Yesterday's gone. We can basically do nothing about it – (but try to mend our mistakes). Tomorrow may never come for us. At least, we don't have that assurance. Today, we're alive and life means change.

Isn't it wonderful that Pope John XXIII threw open the window one day and said, "The Church needs fresh air!" So the old dust flew. Light got into corners that had been hidden from a world that's also dull, and sinful and dusty, and full of crap.

We've all become more aware of the mistakes of the church historically. The Church, dear people, is us! We were made of mud. There's bound to be dust.

Life's not yesterday. We must not sit around and whine about what the Church did to us years ago. Life's today. It's up to us to see to it that our children, in the future of tomorrow, do not look back and whine about what we the Church, Christ's Mystical Body on earth, did today, that caused them harm.

The Church is us. If we don't like something that we see or have memories of, we need to get motivated and help change it.

This is one of the things that the Vatican Council II has done. It has reminded us that the Church is no ecclesiastical authority – "them against us!" It never has been!

We are living in a different era than the last two thousand years. We have change, change; change in our lives today, rapid change. We also have, as in no other time in the history of the world, fast transit and faster communication.

The world is a cold place. The devil and his cohorts lost their light and they want to keep us in darkness. Each of us must protect the light of Christ in us, against the winds and hurricanes of change and times. We must keep our lights glowing so that those around us who are looking for light in the darkness can see and know that there's hope and help available.

## Sixty-Six

## WE ARE THE CHURCH

Let's give the Church a break. It was started by Jesus Christ two thousand years ago. He entrusted it to all who are baptized and placed it under the authority of Peter. His successor is the Holy Father. The Apostles, or Bishops, were His helpers. They are our leaders.

The Church involves us. Together with our leaders, we make up the Mystical Body of Christ on earth today. We are guided by the Holy Spirit Whom Christ sent to strengthen us through the ages. We must quit screaming and writhing and kicking against the goad. If we pull together, harnessed by the Holy Spirit, our efforts would be so much more fruitful.

The Holy Spirit (The love and knowledge of the Father and Son for one another) flows through Christ's Mystical Body, the Church, and here on earth. It flows through a live Body – us. Now you know how wonderful and exciting we each can be. You also know how rotten and sinful we each can be.

Hey, we are the Church. The Church isn't something in the World Book Encyclopedia which we can just look up and admire or scoff at. It's us. You and me, as well as we, are going to be held accountable.

As a very young child, I fell in love with the concept of Bride of Christ. Little did I know that each of us is to be a Bride of Christ. The entire Church is espoused as a Bride to Christ, the Eternal Bridegroom. We have all entered into this eternal espousal at our Baptism. My goal and search has ended at last!

Isaiah 62: 1-5 reads as follows:

"For Zion's sake, I will not be silent. For Jerusalem's sake, I will not be quiet,

Until her vindication shines forth like the dawn and her story like a burning torch,

Nations shall behold your vindication, and all kings your glory.

You shall be called by a new name pronounced by the mouth of the Lord.

You shall be a glorious crown in the hand of the Lord, a royal diadem held by your God.

No more shall men call you "Forsaken" or your land "Desolate,"

but you shall be called "My Delight," and your land "Espoused."

For the LORD delights in you, and makes your land his spouse.

As a young man marries a virgin, your builder shall marry you;

And as a bridegroom rejoices in his bride, so shall your God rejoice in you.

And our response to that is: Thanks be to God!

Our boys now own their Dad's Green Bay Packer tickets.

## Sixty-Seven

## GRADUATIONS AND WEDDINGS

I am now 79 years old. Seventeen years have gone by during which my autobiography has sat on the back of my table. People who have read the first part say it wouldn't be fair not to finish it. Our boys graduated from college. Steve attended the University of Wisconsin at Madison.

He had lived two houses from his future bride on State Street. Her girlfriend would come from Green Bay, and visit and park in the boys' lot. After a while, she would ask, "Would you like to come with me? I'm going over to visit the boys."

Tracy would answer, "No, I better stay here and study. I have a paper that's due."

Steve and Tracy graduated the same day. Her degree was in journalism. His was in business.

The met six months later in a bar in Milwaukee. They discovered that they each knew almost all of the others' friends from high school days in Green Bay.

I've always loved the following story. Tracy had borrowed a lovely sweater from her mother.

She had managed to get a sizeable stain on it. Upon apologizing to her mother, she said, "That's ok, Mom, because I met the man I'm going to marry!"

Tracy, as your mother-in-law, I want you to know that I'm glad you married him! You are a keeper!

Steve and his bride were married in the St. Joseph's College Chapel at St. Norbert's. Beautiful flowers adorned the ends of the pews. A harpist and organist provided ethereal music. Mass was beautiful. A well-known and beloved priest gave a stunning sermon even though he was suffering from laryngitis. Dinner was superb. There were six couples in attendance: four were the bride's brothers; one was Steve's brother Mike. The others were high school friends. Everyone had a great time!

Steve has had several sales jobs which he is good at. He now sells group packages of insurance to large companies.

Tracy is a consultant for toy companies and is very involved in toy fairs throughout the country.

Mike graduated from the University of Wisconsin-La Crosse. He met his girlfriend Michelle from Milwaukee, there. I'm sure she helped and encouraged him through his studies. She later became his wife. Thanks, Michelle! You're a good wife and mother!

Mike sells computer parts to companies throughout Minnesota, the Dakotas and Iowa. Michelle is in charge of a loan group for a Wells Fargo bank in Minneapolis.

Once before he was married, Mike bought a German short hair

puppy and tucked it into his laundry basket. He showed the basket to Michelle and said, "Look what my Mother did to my wash!" From Michelle came a welcome squeal.

The next year they added another German short hair puppy; this became a very big dog.

The two dogs were a very important part of their family for 12 years. At their deaths they were cremated, and their cremains were scattered beside the creek on our woodlot near the cottage, a place we love.

Mike chose a wedding celebration that years ago the Church would have said if any Catholic had attended, they would have committed a mortal sin. I think it was punished by excommunication.

I do know that if Christian charity had been practiced by the priest whom the couple approached, the outcome would have been much different. The priest insisted that the future bride become a Catholic. In this day and age he was on the wrong wavelength.

Instead of gaining a church member he chased two away. Over the passage of years how many of their children will inadvertently follow that path? By that priest's attitude and actions generations of people can be out of the Church fold. This hurts the Church, and it certainly robs its would-be followers of a great treasure.

This situation really upset me because I have seen it happen too often in my life and in the lives of acquaintances.

I know that good priests feel the pain of this also. There has to be a way to heal the great separation between the Church and the millions of people today who are churchless.

Our God is a loving God. He would have searched out these lost sheep and not allowed them to fall off the cliff.

I have great hopes that Pope Francis will be the Christ Light that will brighten our whole world today.

At any rate my son and his beautiful Lutheran bride were married in Minneapolis in a huge aquarium section of a zoo that catered to weddings. The floral display was breathless. Of course we attended.

Fabulous food choices were displayed on a buffet. Hors d'oeuvres were offered by people in tuxedos. A blind man played a synthesizer during the dinner which was followed by a six piece band.

The couple exchanged vows before a non-sectarian woman minister. Behind them, in a huge window the size of a house wall, dolphins played in the water. On another wall, sharks, sea turtles and other ocean denizens frolicked.

Years later, my son and his wife took their sons to the aquarium and explained all this to them. The four year old looked at him sadly and said, "Daddy, why weren't we invited?"

*Sixty-Eight*

## BIRTHS AND BAPTISMS

When our first grandson was about to be born, my son, Steve, called and said, "Mom, in honor of you, we're going to name our baby 'McKinney' and call him 'Mac'."

Mac, Lauren & Ana

That's my maiden name. I went right up in the air. Why would you do that to any human being? His classmates will beat him!

He said, "They'll have to gang up on him if they do. He's already eight and a half pounds. He's not due for two weeks. I thought you'd be honored."

Well, I was, but McKinney Dudkiewicz? The lad has turned out to be quite a young man. At 12, he has had four years of piano lessons. He majors heavily in baseball, basketball, football, and soccer. He's been involved in fencing, wrestling, tennis, skiing and skating and snowboarding. Besides which he is an "A" academic student. He is also a very good human being and a role model <u>for his peers</u>. I am glad they named him McKinney.

My son and his wife are model parents. They sent their children to Montessori for three years before they entered Catholic grade school. Their children have had many sports and leadership camp experiences, and I'm sure their lives will reflect the results of those opportunities.

Steve and his wife, Tracy, also have two stunning daughters. The ten-year old, Lauren, is very musical and artistic. She plays the violin very well for her age. She has had four or five years of different types of dance and gymnastics. Her dance routines amaze us and when she and her father create a routine, it brings tears of joy to our eyes. The girl is as good a human being as she is beautiful. She has an innate confidence that could only have been developed by intelligent, patient parents. She is one of those people whose presence is a soothing balm to any tired, wounded soul.

When Steve knew they were having another baby, he was home for a Packer game. I asked how his wife was. He got all lit up and said, "Well, she's kind of indisposed!"

They had wanted another child for a long time. They hadn't intended to reveal this yet, but he couldn't keep the secret from us. We said, "We won't tell anyone. It's your joy to share."

Just then our second son came in. They had been out taking a stroll with their baby. Mike put the little one on the floor to change his diaper.

Steve says, "Mac and Lauren would like Colton to know that he is going to have a new baby cousin.

Mike looked at his wife, and then said, "Colton would like Mac and Lauren to know that they are going to have a new baby cousin!"

Steve asked when. Mike answered, "June." When Mike asked Steve the same question, he got the same reply, "June".

One came in late May, but they were about three weeks apart.

Steve and Tracy had another little girl, Ana. She absorbs all the qualities of her older brother and sister and recreates them in her own flavor and vivaciousness. She has been carefully taught and cared for and loved by her brother and sister. I don't know how two children could pour more of themselves into a younger sibling than these two have.

Granted the parents work hard on raising and educating this child but the influence of the two older children could not be overestimated. Son and daughter-in-law, your concept of family humbles me.

Steve and Tracy have three children. Each was baptized at St. Peter's Church in East Troy, WI.

The children wore a long white baptismal gown made of handkerchief linen. There are about four five-inch crocheted layers in the skirt. Pink or blue ribbon can be inserted through the upper part of the lace.

A cap and blanket of the same material are decorated with matching ribbon and crocheted lace. The ensemble is gorgeous. It was made for Chet's mother when she had her first child. That would have been at least 95 years ago. By now, close to 100 babies have worn the gown.

When Colton was born, of course we wanted him baptized but I didn't want to aggravate my son. I'd had enough experience with my father not to want to antagonize my son. However, his Lutheran in-laws would not stop bugging him: "When are you going to have that child baptized? When are you going to have that child baptized"?

Mike calls me, "Mom, if we have the baby baptized, can you get into the church?" Arthritis, wheel chair and other health problems have kept me from attending.

I'm thinking, "My getting into church is the least of your worries. There is no chance any priest will baptize him with your background."

Then came the zinger. Mike asked me to make the arrangements. I just wilted. Father will kill me. I don't know this priest!

My other good Catholic son and his wife had to attend classes for six weeks before they'd baptize their baby.

I crawled to the telephone and explained the situation to the pastor whom I didn't know. I told him everything, all of it. His words were: "If the grandparents are faithful parishioners, we will baptize the child."

The week after Christmas, with the church all decorated to celebrate Christ's birth, our baby was baptized. All his Lutheran relatives from 100 miles away were present. Father, I could never thank you enough.

Second baby arrived. For six months, the Lutheran family irritated the parents: "When are you going to get that baby baptized?"

Mike called me, "Ma, I've had it. Will you arrange the baptism?" Once again I wanted to die before begged for another baptism.

I called Father. No questions asked. Parents brought baby from Minneapolis. Lutheran grandparents and family came from Milwaukee. After Mass on Easter Sunday, with the church beautifully decorated to honor the resurrected Christ, our baby was baptized. Thank you Father Tom.

Each baptism has gorgeous pictures to tell the little ones as they grow up that they are children of God. At the time, the boys were 8 months old. They wore beautiful white boy suits.

After each ceremony we all went to a special restaurant. Once I heard myself say, "Don't argue with me. I want to pay the bill." I almost fainted when I saw $499 on the receipt. At least it included the tip!

Any resemblance to the Prodigal Son here? From the arid land of not-much religion, the Church welcomed baby and everyone involved to the Father forever. Son basked in the sunshine of that love at least for a couple days. The infants were freely given the life of sanctifying grade for a starter.

I think the Church should always forgive, heal and welcome.

My mother, a former Protestant, insisted that the indelible mark on our souls at baptism magnetized one back to God through one's lifetime.

I know that God is deeply in my son's heart. If for no other reason, I know that God is in his heart because I'm embedded there.

Every cell of nature reflects God's presence. Both of my sons love nature and reveal its glory to their children.

It seems that in my family history, there are a lot of "checker games" played. As I look back, I think God always wins in His own way.

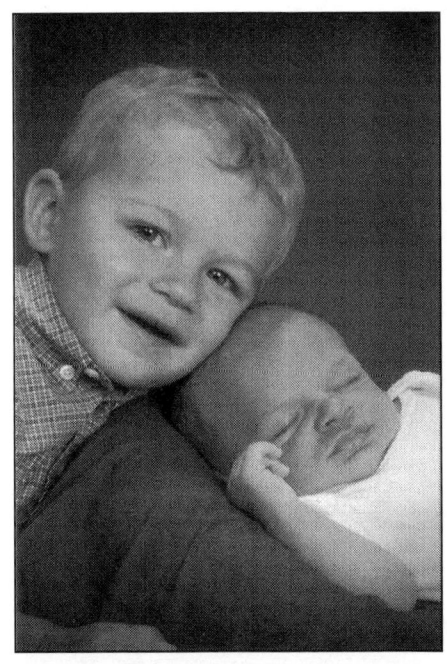

Mike and his wife, Michelle, have two priceless young lads. The first one, Colton, is everyone's dream a-walking. He's gentle, extremely artistic, intelligent, loving, and charming. (I wish people could have said that about me when I was little.) This lad at five is an extreme nature lover who simply has to hunt wintergreen berries every time he comes to the cottage. In season or not, the hunt goes on. He is very protective and concerned about his little brother's well-being even though they fight a lot with each other.

When Griffin was born, Mike called. People do things so differently today. They have labor rooms in which the baby is born. The whole family is sometimes present. There was this super humongous crying. I thought the three year old was there crying. My son said, "Mom, that's our baby!"

Griffin, the baby, is now four years old, and he's gone through every day of his life with that stupendous energy. He's loving, inquisitive and as mischievous as God ever made a little boy.

At Christmas the year he was two, I didn't care if I ever saw the child again. He was obsessed with anything electrical, and you simply could not baby proof the house. Worse yet he was so swift you couldn't keep up with him.

My son and his family left to go to our regular home for a few minutes. I said to my husband, "We'll have to follow them home as soon as we can so he doesn't discombobulate the place."

About fifteen minutes later, I commented to my husband, "It's awfully cold in here." He checked the thermostat and the temperate was down ten degrees. The little guy had followed his mother down to the basement when she put a high chair away. He had flicked off the furnace switch. We were ready to leave. If we hadn't noticed it, all the pipes would have frozen.

My son had left for a football game. He stopped to let the dog in the house and then went to the babysitter's.

We came home, and my husband sat in his chair. Lo and behold, the timer had been pulled out of the wall, and the colored markers were scattered all over the floor.

The next time we saw this little guy, it was summer, and he was no problem. He was in the huge sandbox, running up and down the hills with the big kids or jumping off the docks with the swimmers.

How many 80 year old grandparents have four year old grandchildren? Most by this time have great and great-great grandchildren.

Over the years, at least 60 people were baptized in this gown.

These four people were all baptized in this gown.

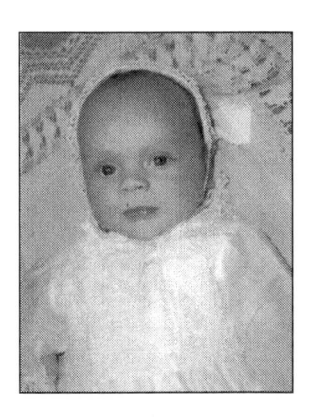

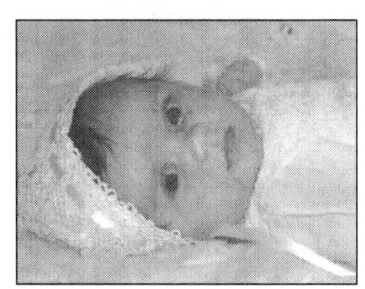

Lauren

Mac

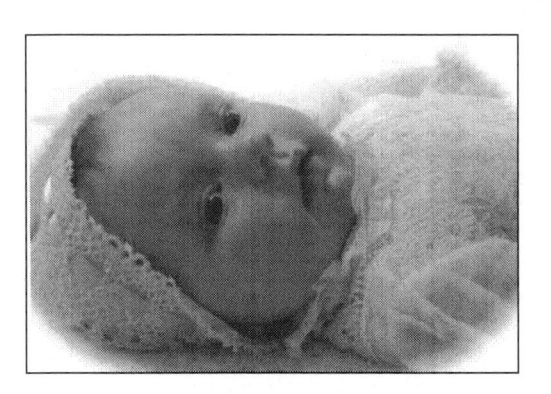

Ana

All baptized at St. Peters in East Troy.

Colton baptized on Easter Sunday.

Griffin baptized two weeks after Christmas
at St. Mary of the Angels in Green Bay.

Arch Bishop Dolan, now Cardinal Dolan, with Mac and Lauren.
It was at Kristyn's confirmation.

## Sixty-Nine

## FUN STORIES NOT TOLD BEFORE

When I was about nine years old, I went out to move my rabbit cage one July morning. There were no rabbits! There were tails and fur.

I ran to my father, "Didn't I move the rabbits last night?"

""Yes, you did," he said.

When I couldn't find them, I thought they had starved to death.

"That's bear fur," he said when he saw what was in the cage. "You ought to write to the game warden."

I did and put a bunch of the hair in the letter, but I didn't tell my father.

Several weeks later Dad came into the house with the warden. "I received your letter, and that is definitely bear fur," the warden said. He explained that the counties reimbursed for bear damage.

"The county is out of money but in the beginning of the year, we'll have more.' he added.

Sure enough in early January I received a check for $24. In 1943, that was a lot of money. Anyway, I was tired of taking care of those rabbits.

But that cage was in my front yard. I didn't think the bear belonged there tearing things apart.

There was a concrete bridge crossing the road of the trout stream where we lived. It was great to sit on the butt of the bridge and fish. I never ever tired of trout fishing. They were such a beautiful shiny fish.

I caught them and threw them up on the bank so I didn't lose them. One time the stream was flooded, and I caught a really big one. When I threw it up the bank, it flopped down and got away.

I remember running barefoot, crying my heart out to Dad who was milking a cow. "Go back and catch it again, you darn fool," he said.

Minutes later I got an even bigger fish. That one I probably pounced on. It was Dad's lesson: "If you don't succeed at first, try against."

Our garden was a long ways from our house and across the creek. There was a spot in the woods called "The Pine Hole". Very few people fished that area.

It was a place on the Eau Claire River where a big pine near the river fell during a storm. Its roots tore a big hole out of the stream bed. It seemed to be a convention place for really big trout.

When gardening or plowing was finished, or I was terribly in need of entertainment, I could almost always enlighten life at "The Pine Hole".

I once took my boys back to the trout stream that I was raised on. I was standing on a tiny island near the beaver dam. I hooked a really large trout. My nine year old son, Mike, thought I needed help. He came running and hit mucky ground. Down he went, feet hitting the base of my isle let, and down I went completely immersed in icy water. The trout waved good-bye and Mike said, "Mom, I've never had more fun in my life!

My brother Roger was nine years older than me. He had once sent for a baby turtle that had Tom mix stamped on its shell. I was probably two or three years old. He took it out of the box and showed it to me. I said, "Oh, Woger, thank you!"

He looked at my mother disgustedly and said, "I suppose she has to have it!"

That's how I got my first turtle.

There was a big gravel pit on our farm. That was the place that I must have learned the joys of water life. I netted minnows and discovered all kinds of insect life. The water would have at least three kinds of dragon fly nymphs. They are called hellgrammites. They're good fishing bait.

I once found a giant water beetle. Its back was completely covered with eggs. The female must lay them on the males back. I certainly backed out of the area quickly. That beetle had claw-like stingers. It can cause tremendous pain.

One time a neighbor who dealt in miscellaneous odds and ends suggested that I catch bullfrogs for frog legs. He'd pay me a certain amount per pound of frog. Well I caught him frogs, zillions of them. The man's name was Hi Edwards.

We kept them in copper boilers and covered wash tubs in the basement. One night Dad had to get up and carry the containers outside because the frogs croaked so loudly that we couldn't sleep!

Dad made Hi pay me before he took the frogs. He transported them from the Antigo-Kempster area, on a hot sunny day to Elkhart Lake in Southern Wisconsin in the back of his pick-up truck in metal containers. Guess what? He whined to my dad about it but dad had protected my part of the deal!

One day I saw a hole in the side of the gravel pit. I put my hand and arm in it. I came to a bend and discovered that I was trespassing. Out torpedoed a kingfisher. It has a beak about 100 inches long! Well, maybe four but it did real damage to me.

I like the look of kingfishers at our lake. They sit prettily and harmlessly on pontoon or dock supports. I saw one dive and get a fish last summer. It was the first time I'd witnessed that. The speed of the dive was unbelievable.

There were a lot of bull frogs in our gravel pit. It was fun to find eggs and hatch pollywogs. However after the frog catching incident the gravel pit wasn't real noisy for several summers.

I loved making dolls both at home and at the cottage. I've made dolls from two inch babies to four foot, size seven dolls. Every one of my dolls was completely made of cloth, body and clothing.

I probably made 300 dolls. Some I sold at craft stores, some I donated to picnics, and some I gave to friends and relatives. Because I had boys, my first set of dolls wore the size two clothes they had outgrown. I loved to make dolls.

One day a lady knocked on my door. In her arms were two dolls wearing my sons' outfits. She had purchased them 32 years before.

"Pat," she said. "These belong to your grandchildren."

Now those dolls wear my grandchildren's clothes. My sons said they were jealous because I had bought the dolls Nike shoes. I couldn't afford them when they were little. They now are assigned to their very own chair in our bedroom, facing the living room.

My other all-consuming hobby is reading. If I get a good novel, I read everything the author wrote. I've been known to read a book two or three times especially if it has a nature background. I love natural science!

When I was a child my dad paid a dime a piece for the three of us to go see a sperm whale that had been brought into Antigo on a railroad freight car.

We went up a set of stairs to sit in a set of table and chairs that were placed in the whale's mouth. I think it had been mounted by a taxidermist. I can still smell the oil dripping into small pails set around the mouth.

I remember my sisters teasing about how it was Dad's way of

introducing me to the world. When he did it for them it only cost three cents apiece. Well, I was very impressed!

Forty years later I took my two young boys to Disney World in Florida. I had to live out Dad's introducing me to the wide world by a different means.

I sent my sons, perhaps five and eight years old, over Disney World in a helicopter. They were scared, excited and exhilarated! They <u>loved</u> it! It damn near killed me to see my two boys and the pilot take off straight up into the air and away! What had I done! What if they crashed? How would I explain that to their Dad? They came back alive and thrilled! For a long time that was their special story to tell!

Almost every year after cold nights in September, we go mushroom-hunting. The ringless honey button kind that we pick grows around dead oak or maple tree stumps. Chet learned to pick them as a child. He taught me and eventually our children to identify them. His parents picked them in Poland.

I cook them in butter and onions and freeze them in cup containers. That way they are ready to throw into roasts, omelets and casseroles. We really love them.

Our son, Michael, has studied mushrooms. He picks several

kinds. If you don't know what you're doing, leave mushrooms strictly alone.

We came up for Valentine's Day this year. Our former contractor plowed out the yard and shoveled a mountain of snow. Griffin, the three year old, went out to meet his daddy at the lake. He actually could have met his maker. He got stuck in the snow, fell and couldn't get up. We thought it was funny but he didn't. It really would have been dangerous if no one was looking out for him. He was yelling, "Daddy, Daddy!"

On the way up from Green Bay, we crossed the Oconto River. It was completely frozen over and covered with snow. About 200 yards down the river, I saw a big buck deer just standing and looking toward the highway. I was so thrilled!

Then the man came to deliver my power wheel chair. I was excitedly telling him about what I had seen.

"Stop", he said, "and let me finish your story. You saw a huge buck deer in the middle of the frozen river. He had seen it several times. It was apparently a DNR decoy. What a way to destroy a vision!

# Seventy

## OUR WOOD LOT AND MAPLE SYRUP

*In* 1980, we bought a 5 acre woodlot. It is about a block from our cottage and is bordered by a creek that is an inlet to the lake.

Chet and I spent months cutting and digging out hazel bushes. We tied red plastic ribbons on all the maple saplings so we wouldn't cut them out once they lost their leaves in full. Without leaves, they were unidentifiable.

The wood lot was cleaned out so that it looked like a park. We worked like slaves just because it was fun! We raked it and hauled all the brush and leaves to the stream shore. In winter, the ten-foot piles began to decay and compress. In spring, the deer had a feast. They ate almost all our maple saplings. There went our future maple syrup forest! If we hadn't chopped and dug out the other brush, the maple wouldn't have been so visible, and it would have had a chance to grow up. Actually a lot of maple did grow.

At any rate, we love the woodlot just for its beauty and accessibility. It has provided huge piles of wood that has been split for pits and fireplaces.

We've spent thousands of hours over the years trying to keep ahead of Mother Nature. Just when we had it looking like a park, along came a cyclone and knocked down 26 huge trees. When we got that cleaned up, Oak Wilt Disease came and destroyed all our oaks.

I transplanted 13 hemlocks into the lot. I think the deer thought they were made of candy. Every spring, they'd chomp what grew to the ground.

Mike loves the wood lot. In summer, he mows it and hauls brush. In late fall, he tries to keep up with all the dead trees. Mike always keeps the road open so that I can drive around in my scooter.

Huge piles of brush are burned in winter.

Mike, in case you don't know it (ha ha), we deeply appreciate all the hard work you've put in the woodlot. It's good to see our love for the woods reflected in you.

One time a male cougar also known as a mountain lion, puma or panther, was sitting in the entrance of the woodlot, staring out at a passer-by as if to declare the land his own. These animals have about a 50 mile radius or territory so I probably won't ever see him.

I have wished, and wished and wished to see him but he's never there for me. He's been seen twice. I have an ax and a metal whistle in my scooter basket just in case I need it! I know that's laughable – so laugh!

The most exciting things that we see in the woodlot are deer, turkey, and bird nests.

I like to drive the car into the woodlot. That way I collect less woodticks! I read a book and listen to the sounds.

The frogs in the creek and swamp on the other side make so much noise you wish that you could clamp their vocals shut.

Bitterns add their loud whampa, whampa. All you can see of them is their long beak sticking straight up from their nests.

Sand hill cranes fill the air with their cerock-cerock call.

Geese nest along the creek. Wood ducks fill box nests made for them. They also nest in the holes of dead wood. This is just what I'm aware of. I'm sure that there's much more life of which I am unaware.

Our sons were children when we had all eight of the cousins each hide nine wrapped packages of Halloween candy in the woodlot. The only rule was that some part of the wrapping had to show. It could be in a tree, stump, a hole, in the ground, hanging from a bush, etc. That made 72 packages.

At midnight, we all went out for tricks or treats with a flashlight. The children couldn't even remember where they each hid their treats because the night world was so different than daylight. Talk about fear and fun! The kids had heard coyotes howling at night. They didn't know coyotes wouldn't be out with noisy people around! Besides, grown up dads were making animal noises!

One mother brought her huge Airedale dog along (a bear hunter) because she was afraid of what was in the dark!

Our grandchildren haven't been around for Halloween but they sure have had fun with Easter egg hunts in the woodlot!

When I was a child, my father and an uncle made maple syrup. I spent several entire nights with them where there was an abundance of maple trees.

We collected sap by driving a team of horses hitched to a stone boat. This was a triangle of split logs. We carried milk cans full of sap back to the cooking vat.

I remember it being long, boring hard work. What's more I didn't like maple syrup. It was too thin. I liked my mother's homemade brown sugar syrup with butter in it.

60 years later, when Chet said, "I should get some taps and show the boys how to make maple syrup; I remembered what hard work it was! I distinctly remember my answer: "For God's sake, Chet, don't start that!" Besides, Chet knew nothing about it!

So five, 16, 30, 40 taps later, Chet is in full swing. He says the way hunters get buck fever, he gets sap fever. No matter how you skin this, for an amateur maple syrup maker, it's an exhausting labor of love.

My husband explained what he does, and I wrote all his words down:

Taps are placed at a 45-degree angle up into a tree. A 3/8 inch bit is used to drill the hole about 1½ to 1¾ inch into the tree to support the pail and capture the sap. Sap flows between the tree's bark and cambium. It flows up in the morning and down at night. This is so it doesn't freeze.

Sap flows best after a freezing night and a warm 40-degree day. There can be between five and 15 good running days. A season might go from one to five weeks. During that time a tree can produce very little or as much as 16 gallons.

I gather the sap whenever I get 35 to 40 gallons or within 72 hours of flow time. After that the sap sours and is no good.

Chet and Mac making maple syrup.

My stainless steel boiling pan holds 35 gallons which equates to a gallon of early run syrup. This should turn out to be clear amber after straining it through felt.

Boiling is started early in the morning when there is less wind. I don't boil when there is rain or snow. I started with a rolling fire and temper it with the embers at the end to prevent the batch from burning.

The sap is reduced to two or three gallons in the big pan, then transferred to a five gallon steel pan to finish the boiling process before canning. The temperature at this point should be 210 degrees.

I usually have about 720 gallons of sap during a season which equates to about 80 pints.

Our grandchildren won't eat any syrup but Grandpa's. Our sons bring their children to help carry sap and watch the process.

This seems like a lot of sap but every year is not a good run. Year 2013 was a banner year. Best ever, people said.

However, since Chet broke his leg in December, 2012, he wasn't up to the rigors of walking around on snow and ice. He collects his sap by hand, carrying it in pails. At 80 years old, this is not an easy task.

So now we're into 2014. Chet's really been slowed up by his broken leg, however the fever is still invading his blood stream. I don't know how he could possibly make syrup any more, but I know he's dreaming!

Our last jar of maple syrup!

# Seventy-One

## TRYING TO DULL THE PAIN

*I* don't really know what caused the net disaster. I am diabetic and would wake up during the night restless and hungry. Eating something would let me go back to sleep.

I always had our fireplace decorated to the best of my ability. I had a pair of hand-carved, life sized cardinals watching over a grapevine nest with four wooden eggs. I prized these, watched that no child violated them.

One night while speaking in a stupor to my husband, I sat on them! It was during one of my night excursions. Then I got up, laid on my husband's side of the bed and went to sleep.

Soon after, I woke up with terrible carpal tunnel pain. I got up, shook my hands out and went to the kitchen for some food. Granted, it wasn't on my diabetic diet. When I was finished, to save energy and the need to walk back to the light switch, I turned off the light. There was a full moon, and the neighbors' yard light provided some semblance of light.

I reached up high to put my snack away and completely lost my sense of balance. There was nothing to grab onto without breaking it. Down I went, breaking me. I hit a metal table, breaking my glasses. I ended up on my face under the kitchen table. I discovered that falling on ceramic tile is not a comfortable landing!

My husband called the ambulance which came very quickly considering that we are out in the country. I broke the ball of my shoulder in three pieces. My upper arm was in a very jagged, complete break.

The emergency room doctor said it couldn't have a cast on account of the weight that would be dragging on the shoulder. He said it would always be stiff. What he didn't say was that it would always, always hurt. But it does!

At the same time I jammed my knees, which for years had been bone on bone. I had in the past gone to several other orthopedic doctors who would say, "How are you walking on those knees? They're bone on bone. They can go backward as well as forward."

No one would risk the surgery. The excuses at first were, "You're too young. They'll only last 15 years. You're too heavy. They'll break out."

Well, 30 years later I'm still walking on them. Every step hurts unbelievably. Once again, the St. Louis de Montfort vow: all is offered to Jesus through Mary for where it is needed most on earth. And, brother, does the earth need it according to any news report here and abroad.

The broken arm resulted in my being in a nursing home for a month. We definitely had disagreements with the administration but years later as I look back at it; it was all in all a pleasant experience. I loved the residents. We had a lot of fun together, and I hated to leave some of them.

Now the pain which never disappeared kept increasing. One time the emergency room sent me to a pain clinic.

There I had a vivacious woman doctor whom I loved. She gave me shots in my knees made from rooster combs that didn't help. I had electrical gadgets that wrapped around my legs all night to regenerate collagen in my knees. Didn't work. She gave me opiate drugs until I was under five of them, and I mean under! Each time I went, they took all my pills from me and counted everyone I had taken, I was using exactly what the doctor had prescribed. I knew that they were causing euphoria.

One time I was in the bathroom and looked at the tub. I thought, "Man, would a tub bath feel wonderful!" I hadn't been able to get into a tub for years, but in I went. Talk about Paradise! I drained the water and attempted to get out. It was a no go!

Nothing we did worked; I had three grab bars readily at my disposal. We were about to call for the fire department for assistance when my husband had the most innovative thought. He came with an armful of investment yearly book reports. We always teased him when numerous black plastic covered reports came in. I wanted to laugh at him. He was thinking so hard that I could see smoke coming out of his ears.

"Pat," he said, "try putting these under each cheek, one at a time, to build yourself up. I thought that he was crazy but lo and behold, it worked! Finally with the grab bars and his helping hand, up I came. I haven't tried that trick since. However, a fireman that we knew later said we should have filled the tub to the top. It would have been buoyant!

I praised and praised my husband's ingenuity. He was my hero in shining armor! And then, according to my version, and his chagrin and embarrassment, the next day he ran over me with his car.

By now, you're catching on to the fact that those pain drugs were inebriating me. My husband backed the car out of the garage. I remember thinking he was driving awfully fast. By now I was across the driveway. It never entered his mind that I could move fast enough to be outside yet. He was watching the other direction so as not to hit the chimney. My perception of his speed was due to pills.

Gas at that time was very expensive. I thought, "He'll stop there and get out. I'll step right in and no gas will be wasted."

I stepped forward, thinking I knew right where he would stop. Only he didn't, and the side view mirror hit me. Having no balance, my canes flew into the neighbors' bushes, and I reluctantly followed, cussing of course.

My husband was sitting with his feet out of the car, his head in his hands, saying, "Oh, no! Oh, no."

I yelled, "Quit moaning about this and get me up before I stiffen solid."

All's well that ends well in this case. He picked me up off the grass, retrieved my canes, and I drove off to get my medicine renewed.

This went on for several more months, and the doctor said, "I've been working with you for a whole year, and I haven't been able to change your pain. I'm going to give you a real cocktail. If it causes you any trouble, let me know." When trouble came, I didn't know about it! I was in another world!

Now she added this so called "cocktail" on top of the five different opiates that I was taking. Other doctors' reports said that these drugs did not metabolize, but collected in my brain. About three days later, I started a four week stint of hallucination hell.

I woke up one morning, and there were people living in my cupboards. I was angry at my husband for letting them dry my dishes.

For four weeks nothing I thought happened did. Anything that did happen wasn't comprehended as real. I still remember all the monumental scenes as if they were happening today.

The hospital in Green Bay sent me to Froedert Hospital in Milwaukee. If they had sent me by helicopter I would be upset to this day as I remember nothing of the journey. At least it was by ambulance. Most of what happened there I don't remember. But I could write a book on the indescribable hallucinations. None of them were violent except one where I was defending myself. All the rest were beautifully colored artisan dreams.

After a few days, they took me out of ICU. That night in my hallucinations, I left the hospital, and walked through the most beautifully misty grounds to someone's house.

Their lake-colored walls were all somehow partly alive. Huge ceramic fish (or were they real?) moved all around the walls like they were swimming. They were brightly colored, unlike anything I had ever seen.

In one room, the floor was like that. It was tiled. Maybe 10 large fish that were raised only two inches from the floor swam at will. You had to walk gingerly so as not to trip on them.

It was a crazy but beautiful world! While at Froedert, among other adventures, I thought I drove my husband's car 200 miles away to wonderful familiar woods where hundreds of land turtles were mating. I can still smell the fecundity of the swamp moss. Every swamp plant and flower that I knew was blossoming. I collected eight pairs of different turtles for my sons to each have in their own ponds. One set even had square shells!

I was so angry every time someone told me that what was so real to me didn't exist. My husband's leg was on fire. There was a huge manhole cover on the floor in my room. There was a hog nose snake on the window sill. All kinds of obnoxious plants grew in the corner of my room. Everybody would say no, that wasn't true. I could see the damn things! What was wrong with those people!

I was at Froedert Hospital for ten days, driving everyone else crazy. They finally thought they had my brain flushed out. They sent me home, and a week later I was back in a local hospital. I was there a week, and they sent me home as okay.

Shortly thereafter I was back. I remember thinking that I was in a huge, cool dairy. From all the ceilings thousands of tiny fishing hooks hung down almost at head level. It disturbed me terribly. What a thing to go on in a dairy! I kept trying to get rid of them.

I was sent to Brown County Mental Hospital. After a week, they sent me home.

Once more I was hauled to the local hospital. They must have said, "Oh, no, not her again."

So, once again, they shipped me back to the mental hospital, this time in the back of a cop car. The mental floor at the hospital didn't have room for me.

My son said, "Let me ride with her. She'll be traumatized in a cop car."

That nice cop asked if I'd feel better if he drove around the block a couple times a night to keep the people out of my cupboards. I was so pleased for that security!

While at the Mental Hospital, I convinced my son to accompany me while I filled out a formal complaint with police that I had been raped by a man who said his name was "Cat Man." Then I realized that couldn't have occurred. It happened right after I had pushed a 100-foot motor home single handedly across a huge meadow and over a cliff, killing another man.

That was when reality took over hallucinations.

Once more I was released from the Mental Hospital. In the process of leaving, two different psychiatrists said that I had shown no sign of mental illness.

Twice before, psychiatrists told me that when I went for counseling. My sincere curiosity says, "What on earth do they use for criteria? How can they tell?" At any rate, thanks be to God.

Once the opiates were flushed out of my brain, I have no longer had mental problems.

I'm sure many people would have sued the doctor. People thought I should have. I know that she was chastised by the medical community that investigated the situation for the amount she had given me.

I liked the doctor. She had tried to help me. I never went back to her but if I had the opportunity, I would like to be her friend or neighbor.

As each of us age, physical problems occur. Pope John Paul II did a marvelous thing when he stayed Pope until death. He had tremendous physical problems but his mind was still clear and brilliant. He remained as Pope, he said, through all his illness to show the world that there was dignity in the old age of life.

Before this book is published, John Paul II will be canonized as a Saint. He certainly has my greatest admiration. I don't have enough words in my vocabulary to express how he has buoyed up my spirit as I become elderly.

There were very few of the indecencies of old age that Pope John Paul did not endure, besides having been shot years earlier.

It takes real humility to accept all the help that age can demand. Until you reach that stage, you will never truly understand. <u>Never</u>.

Youth simply will never be able to fathom age. It's a good thing because if they did, they wouldn't have the courage to enter the journey. It is definitely not for the faint hearted.

My physical pain often puts John McCain in mind. He suffered so much in Korean prisons. I often find myself thinking, "If John McCain could do this, so can I"! I thank him for that leadership. It has nothing to do with politics – it's simply his leadership gift to humanity!

I realize that John McCain may not even be aware of his light in the darkness. However it is there for people to see.

# Seventy-Two

## A NEW DREAM EMERGES

During the time that these episodes took place, much else occurred. My husband had his own personal dream.

We had a very nice but compact cottage. For 32 years it was comfortable. The walls were all knotted pine with white acoustic tile ceilings throughout. It consisted of a kitchen, a living room with a "warm morning" space header and a small bathroom. We had no hot water. There were two small bedrooms.

The cottage was sufficient for us because when we were younger and our sons were young, we were always outside. We locked the doors in the early morning until everyone was dressed, breakfast and dishes were taken care of and beds were made. Then the doors were opened, and we all went out together. It had to be that way because we were 75 feet from the lake and our children were four and not yet one. Our eyes had to be on them all the time.

Once we ran the shorelines, calling for 4 year old Steve. He was hiding in the outhouse. We should have known that he couldn't have gotten to the lake. He had just been beside us. But our hidden fears of a drowning overtook both of us instantly.

Anyway, the four-year old's humor just took over. It was fun to see Mom and Dad running and yelling their heads off while he watched them. We were tearfully assured that nothing like that would happen again.

So the old cottage needed a new roof and siding as we never wanted to paint it again. We also needed a garage. It was now 2002.

My husband drew plan after plan after plan. A large maple tree was causing him frustration because it was blocking development. It was a prime sap producer for making maple syrup in spring.

It had huge yellow leaves in fall. They all seemed to come down at once. When the kids were little, they loved to roll around and hide in the huge leaf piles. The tree also provided shade for the cottage.

It was such a problem because building restrictions on the lake are so stringent. A building has to be 75 feet from the lake and 25 feet from another lot. One side can be ten feet and the other, 15.

Chet drew blueprints in his sleep, I think. It seemed that he would have to build up –a two story living area. However, we knew that aging would make climbing stairs difficult for both of us.

Finally Chet discovered rot in the trunk. Down came the tree. This was sad because we loved it but the decision freed the floor plans.

All the time our sons figured nothing would come of it. At one time or another, each son said to me, "Mom, I can't stand to listen to it."

We had a contractor who simply loved the plan. What a mansion unfolded! It is 2,600 sq. ft. They started in December and we were finished in April.

As the building began to progress, Steve asked to have input. Well, there wasn't an inch of the building that he didn't okay or revise. As he said, "Dad, you're spending part of the money that you said you were saving for us. Make the place so we will be proud of it 50 years from now."

Mike said, "You don't want to have too many people involved in this. Do whatever you want. Just don't paint it purple."

Both sons have been amazed at what has transpired from Dad's plans. Anyone would be proud of it 50 years from now. It is no longer a cottage. When we are well, it's our primary home. We will always be grateful for Chet's serious, serious planning! And Steve, even though our old heads didn't always see eye to eye with your young head – we thank you for your input!

When we're not well or just need a couple night's stay, we have a home in town. It's small, accessible and very nice to have. It's also close to hospitals and medical care.

It seems there should be more words to describe our cottage but words can't. It's the living in it and the memories that give it the glow of life.

Should have made a 3-stall garage!

Oh, for the warmth of that fireplace!

## Seventy-Three

## GRADUALLY WINDING DOWN

*S*wimming in summer is a constant activity. No sooner are they out, they get something to eat, and back they go. People are in the water from 8:00 a.m. to 10:00 p.m.

The neighbor has a water trampoline that is a huge attraction.

There are many kayaks on the lake. Sometimes it looks like a rainbow; there are so many different colors. People often go kayaking on the Peshtigo River.

Wild Grapes. Last summer I came upon wild grapes while I was out with my scooter. They were close to the road, but over a slight ditch.

The vines grew up into trees. I pulled them down and stripped off the grapes, filling a gallon bucket.

It came time to leave and my scooter said, "You got me in here. How do you expect to get out?"

A car came by and I waved a weak "Help me!" Car passed.

I was thinking unkind words. Then I grabbed a metal whistle that I always carry with me. I blew it hard. The car was about two blocks away. It stopped. I was still cussing! A nice young man came running back. With a lot of effort of my getting off the scooter on uneven ground, and his hard energy, the scooter came out of the ditch.

The man's parting words were, "Whatever you do, young lady, keep that whistle on you!" Later, those grapes made wonderful juice.

The last four years have gone along fairly smoothly. Health will always be concern. This last Thanksgiving evening, we put up our beautiful artificial balsam tree at the cottage. Everyone helped decorate it in colored lights and red balls. It was covered with 50 three-inch tan teddy bears. Ninety hand crocheted snowflakes made by a niece many years ago complemented the deep green tree.

When my niece sent the snowflakes, a note said: "Aunt Pat, I can't express my emotions easily but this is to show you how I've always felt about you." That, dear niece, was read through tears.

Our dining room wall had a four-foot tree that was gorgeously decorated in maroon and gold. A friend had taken a regular tree and pushed all the branches forward. It was a beautiful wall tree.

We were all ready to celebrate Christmas Eve before the fireplace. All the grown-ups and kids would be there – we thought.

On December 9, 2012, Chet went downstairs on a simply innocent task. He was going to cover the basement windows with plastic for the winter.

Somehow he missed the bottom step. He doesn't remember what happened.

Four feet in front of him was the outside wall of the recreation room. He could have easily broken his neck. In his hand he had a sharp scissors and tape. He didn't cut himself but he did break both bones in his right leg above the ankle.

I'm handicapped. He didn't call out for help but came up on his butt step by step. Somehow, upon getting upstairs, he dragged himself up onto a chair.

"911?" I said. He said, "Don't you dare! "Ok", I replied. So the next morning he looked at his swollen, purple leg and let his niece take him to the hospital. I don't know if you'd call him a trooper or an idiot, but he survived. However his life has slowed down. Chet's niece Kathy did our grocery shopping. I tried to help Chet as much as I could. It was a long winter.

Besides his broken legs, flu invaded other people's plans, but we all survived the holidays. When we returned to the cottage on Memorial Day, our house was exquisitely decorated for Christmas.

The Fourth of July brought another great cottage celebration last summer. Everyone had great fun swimming, fishing, eating by the fire pit and watching fireworks. I wasn't feeling well and didn't seem to know it. I lashed out at Steve, "I might as well be dead. You're all running around having fun. No one seems to know I'm here!"

I was certainly out of the flow of things. We all went home the next day. When I left, I just knew that I'd never see the cottage again, and what was worse, I didn't care.

Several nights later I put down a book I was reading. Either I was awfully tired, or it didn't make sense. My husband said, "You'd better test your blood sugar." He brought me the kit which I used four times a day. I didn't know what it was for or how to use it. He called an ambulance.

I was beginning to have a stroke. Because I got to St. Vincent hospital so fast, they were able to stop it. By the time my husband got to the hospital, I didn't even know who *he* was.

My heart was not a happy heart, four arteries were blocked. One was 98 percent; the others were between 80 and 90 percent blocked.

I had four stents implanted. These are like tiny culverts put into an artery to keep it open so that blood can flow through. One clot is still in the heart. Nothing can be done surgically. Medication will have to take care of that.

Several times my heart rate was 34 times a minute. So now I'm taking lifetime medications. No wonder I was once more questioning my existence.

For the last month a hospital program has sent a nurse, a physical therapist and an occupational therapist to my home twice a week. They've been superlatively wonderful. I'm sad to see the need for them ending.

One of the wonderful things that happened when I was in the

hospital was being visited by five members of my former religious community. They were classmates. An 85 year old, an 83 year old, a 79 year old and a 78 year old all had tears streaming down our faces. How could this be? We still felt like kids. I hadn't seen some of these people in 50 years.

The hospital's program I'm under keeps me homebound. So we couldn't go to the cottage for Labor Day. My husband couldn't go because health-wise someone has to be with me.

All was fairly acceptable until one of my sons called and said that they were all up at the cottage. They didn't let us know they were going because they thought we would feel bad that we couldn't go.

They were right! It hit like a sledge hammer. The fact that everybody but us were at the cottage portends the future. We remodeled it with them in mind, and soon they'll take over. Eighty-year olds don't live forever.

So this brings to an end the saga up to 2014. It's been a good life. Tears and sorrow come in all lives but my wonderful husband of 45 years and my sons have made my life truly worth living. Thank you, as you have so often thanked me for the decisions in my life that has allowed your lives to exist!

Only God knows how long our lives will last. I have a poster that says, "80 is the new 50!" That remains to be seen.

We sadly missed Labor Day, but we've since had a wonderful Christmas at the cottage. We will soon be spending the bulk of our time there, God willing.

If we live healthily, long enough, we plan on spending our 45th wedding anniversary there in July.

Hopefully these books will be printed by then.

One morning this last December, I was walking into the kitchen with my quad and hemi canes. My right knee went out. I hit my head on a hard maple table before landing under it.

I'm on Coumadin, a blood thinner; therefore I needed to go to the hospital. Tests did not show bleeding in the brain. However, my knees will no longer let me walk.

I was sitting in my recliner one evening when the motor went out leaving me with my legs up in the air.

I called Green Bay home Medical who have always been most accommodating. Several men came and tipped my chair forward while holding on to me.

I had been sleeping in the recliner at night because I couldn't walk into my bedside.

They brought me an electric bed. I have used a sleep apnea machine for over 20 years. With the aid of the above two, I get very good night's rest.

Bob Murphy from Green Bay Home Medical and Dr. Joseph Dobson has managed to get me an electric motorized wheel chair for the cottage-home which will make life a lot easier. Soon it will be our primary home. Chet has a niece who has helped us beyond belief through our handicaps. She did all our shopping and transporting for months when Chet's leg was broken. Kathy Kaminski, God will surely reward you for all you do for so many people!

Nurses came from the hospital 3 days a week for 6 weeks after I came home from the hospital. I have hired a lady to help in the house one day a week. I don't believe I could have found a better match than Mary.

Another lady, Lisa Devroy, has made these books possible by her expertise, encouragement, and typing! She has certainly been a Godsend.

My husband, Chet, deserves all the credit in the world. He does daily wound care and bathing. He helps me maneuver around a potty chair. That must seem like a hundred times a day as I am on four water pills.

I'm not crying about my situation. I'm just demonstrating that I know what I'm talking about when I speak of the vicissitudes of old age. We will all get there if we live long enough! Be prepared and bring along your sense of humor! You will need it!

- *Pat*

## *Acknowledgements*

To Kathy Kaminski, our dear niece, who has called us every day, run errands and in general been a life line. Thank you! Thank you! Thank you!

As a child looks **forward into life**, I am giving my life a cursory **backward glance**. I love this picture. Lilly scooted behind the trellis just as the picture was snapped. Everyone thought that she ruined the snapshot until it was developed.

Isn't it gorgeous?
To me it symbolizes all aspects of life, youth, middle age, and senior life.

*God bless and guide us all!*

Made in United States
Orlando, FL
10 December 2022